The Way of the Kingdom

A Call to Live from Heaven's Perspective

by Nathan Dennis

"But seek first the kingdom of God
and his righteousness,
and all these things will be added to you."
— *Matthew 6:33 (ESV)*

ISBN: 979-8-218-83000-7

To my Dad and Mom,

who showed me Jesus not only in what you said but in how you lived. Your faith was steady, your love unwavering, and your lives pointed me toward the reality of His Kingdom. I am who I am today because of the way you lived for Him.

Contents

Introduction: The Kingdom We Were Made For

"But seek first the Kingdom of God and His righteousness, and all these things will be added to you." — Matthew 6:33 (ESV)

There is a Kingdom that transcends every tribe, denomination, and culture.
It isn't confined by stained glass or steeples. It is not built by human hands, nor is it sustained by political power, religious effort, or personal charisma.

This Kingdom cannot be shaken because it wasn't formed on earth.
It is the Kingdom of God and once you see it, nothing else will satisfy.

When Leading Isn't Enough

I've spent much of my life leading in the Church preaching sermons, planting ministries, building teams, leading worship, and helping people walk through both joy and sorrow. I have always endeavored to be all in. Passionate. Sincere. Committed.

And yet, despite all that outward activity and some "success", something in me began to ache. Not burnout. Not disillusionment.

Hunger.

I started noticing patterns I could no longer ignore. It felt like people were coming but not changing. We were preaching truth, but lives weren't being transformed. There was structure but not surrender. Activity, but not authority. We had created something people could attend, but not necessarily something they could *become*.

We produced services, not disciples.

Somewhere along the way, I realized I had learned how to lead well without always knowing how to live fully.

And so, I began to ask a dangerous, but sincere question:

If we're doing everything right, why isn't it producing the fruit Jesus promised?

That question led me into a season of deep reflection and reevaluation. I returned to Scripture with new eyes. I tried to listen less to strategies and more to the Spirit of the Lord. What I discovered wasn't that I had lost my way, I had simply outgrown a system. What I was really longing for wasn't just a better model of Church. I was longing for the Kingdom.

Not theory. Not tradition. Reality.

Jesus as King. His presence, His reign, His way.

A Wake-Up Call

This book is the fruit of that journey. It's not meant as a critique of the Church, it's a call back to her true identity.

It's not a leadership manual. It's not seven keys to growth or a Christian self-help plan. It's a wake-up call to the life Jesus actually offered: a life where He is central, where community is real, and where freedom invades every corner of how we live.

The Kingdom Jesus preached is wild, beautiful, unshakable, and completely unlike anything the world can manufacture. It flips tables. It heals the broken. It calls out the fake. It refuses performance and invites transformation.

God is awakening His people in this generation—not just to talk about the Kingdom, but to live it.

He's calling us out of dead religion and into vibrant relationship.
Out of cultural conformity and into radical obedience.
Out of comfort and into commission.

This is not about improving the Church you attend.
It's about becoming the reflection of the King and His Kingdom here and now.

Why These Seven Priorities?

The seven priorities in this book aren't exhaustive, but they are essential. They've been forged through Scripture, tested in real life, and sharpened through the voices of Kingdom-minded leaders like T. Austin-Sparks, Watchman Nee, N.T. Wright, Dan Mohler, Frank Viola, and many others who have refused to settle for domesticated Christianity and the status quo.

Each chapter will press against the grain of cultural Christianity and invite you into something deeper—something more glorious and costly. You'll discover:

1. Why Jesus isn't just your Savior—He's your center
2. How man-made religion can distort the Gospel and how to break free
3. Why discipleship thrives in authentic community, not isolated belief
4. How to resist the gravitational pull of the world's systems
5. What radical grace and true repentance look like in real life
6. Why mission is not a trip—it's your new normal
7. How to read Scripture through the lens of the King and His Kingdom

These are more than teachings or ideas. They are keys not to a method, but to a mindset; a whole new way of seeing and being. A Kingdom mindset. A transformed life.

Come Hungry

If you've felt it too, if you've sensed that there must be more than services, more than effort, more than polished spirituality then you're not alone. And you're not crazy.

You're being called.

This book won't entertain you. It might wreck you in the best way. It might shake loose what's shallow and stir up what's sleeping. But if you'll let it, it will point you back, not to a system, but to a Savior.

Welcome to the Way of the Kingdom. This is the path you were made for. Let's walk it together.

Chapter 1: Christ-Centered Living

**Jesus is not just Savior. He is Lord.
He is King. He is Everything.**

"Why do you call me 'Lord, Lord,' and don't do the things I say?"
— *Luke 6:46*
"But we see Jesus..." — *Hebrews 2:9 (NKJV)*
"He is before all things, and by him all things hold together."
— *Colossians 1:17*

---

*So what does it really mean to live the Kingdom
and not just believe in it from a distance?
True Kingdom life starts at the feet of Jesus.
That's where everything is re-centered.
Let's start with the first and most essential reality.
Christ at the center.*

Here is the problem. We often get the focus wrong. Instead of fixing our eyes on Jesus, we prioritize other things like the music, the production, the vibe of the room, or the metrics of ministry success. We measure how powerful a moment was by the response it got, not the presence it carried. But hear me: anything — and I do mean anything — we place at the center that isn't Christ is the wrong aim. When the center shifts, everything else follows. And a misplaced center leads to a misplaced life. Christ-centered living doesn't just mean believing in Jesus, it means building everything around Him. The Kingdom begins where self, success, and spectacle step aside and Jesus takes His rightful place.

A Kingdom Without a King?

Many believers today live as if Jesus is the mascot of their lives not the monarch. He's celebrated but not enthroned. Consulted, but not obeyed. We want His presence to comfort us but not confront us.

The Kingdom of God isn't an *accessory* you put on; it stands firm on our *allegiance*.

The Kingdom isn't a democracy we vote on, or a co-op we negotiate. It is not a hobby we add to our schedule. It is a Kingdom, and it begins where the Lordship of Christ is embraced without condition.

Jesus didn't come to renovate your life. He came to rebuild it entirely. He didn't come to improve your story. He came to end it and raise you into His.

The Christian life isn't about inviting Jesus into your world; it's about dying to self and coming alive in Him.

To live the Kingdom is to live with Jesus at the center. The center of your affections, the center of your identity, the center of your priorities and the center of your moments.

When Ministry Took the Spotlight

There was a season in my life when everything on the outside looked right. Our church was growing, and the services were full. I was working hard and staying faithful. But somewhere underneath the motion was a subtle drift.

I started noticing there was a huge difference between talking about Jesus and being with Him.

After one particularly "successful" Sunday, I lingered in the empty sanctuary. Lights dimmed. Music silenced. And for the first time in a long time, I noticed the hollowness in my own soul. I had become so busy pointing people toward Jesus that I had lost sight of Him myself.

That moment didn't produce shame—it produced clarity.

It wasn't a feeling that I was failing, instead I realized I was being invited. Invited to come back to simplicity, back to wonder, and back to the Center.

"The greatest tragedy in the Church is not her lack of influence—it's her loss of center. Christ is not a ministry tool. He is the reason we breathe."
– Frank Viola

Seeing Jesus in Everything

Hebrews 12:2 says to *"keeping our eyes on Jesus, the pioneer and perfecter of our faith."*

That's not a poetic encouragement. It's a spiritual survival tactic.

When we take our eyes off Jesus, we drift. But when we behold Him, we're transformed (2 Corinthians 3:18). This is why Paul declared, *"I resolved to know nothing... except Jesus Christ and Him crucified"* (1 Corinthians 2:2). Not because he lacked wisdom, but because Jesus *is* wisdom. Not because he lacked depth, but because Christ is the depth.

We never grow beyond Jesus.
We only grow deeper *into* Him.

A Christ-centered life isn't one where Jesus gets the first slice of our schedule. It's where He becomes the substance of every slice—our thoughts, our time, our interactions, our rest, our relationships.

Jesus Is Not a Brand

In today's culture, it's all too easy to reduce Jesus to a brand, a logo, or a marketing strategy. He's quoted on Instagram, printed on t-shirts, and hash tagged into our content. But Jesus is not a concept to be marketed—He is a Person to be known.

He is not a spiritual accessory we add to make life more meaningful.
He is not a life coach, a feeling, or a mascot for our agendas.
He is the King of Glory, the Son of God, and the Living Christ—real, present, and personal.

You don't build a relationship with a brand.
You don't commune with a concept.
But you can walk with Jesus, hear His voice, be moved by His presence, and live in step with His Spirit.

Colossians 1:27 states that it is "Christ in you, the hope of glory."
Read that again it's not Christ beside you. Not Christ as your label. It is Christ *in* you.

The world doesn't need a better Christian brand that is palatable to popular culture and easy to market to the masses.

It needs people who are so saturated with the real presence of Jesus that everything about them smells like Heaven.

Christ: The Revealer of the Father

Some people fear that placing too much focus on Jesus somehow diminishes the revelation of the Father heart of God. But nothing could be further from the truth. To center your life on Christ is not to ignore the Father, it is to see Him more clearly. Jesus is the full revelation of God.

"The one who has seen me has seen the Father." — John 14:9
"He is the image of the invisible God.." — Colossians 1:15
"The Son is the radiance of God's glory and the exact expression of his nature..." — Hebrews 1:3

If you want to know what God is like, look at Jesus. He is not a chapter in the story. He *is* the story. The full character, heart, and nature of the Father are revealed through the Son. To be Christ-centered is to be biblically centered because it is through Jesus that we see the Father and receive the Spirit.

We don't need to toggle between divine persons based on what we need—comfort from the Father, fire from the Spirit, or direction from the Son. In Jesus, we get the fullness of God. This is not a competition but communion, where Christ is the face of that communion with us.

Jesus-Focused, Not Spirit-Fragmented

In recent years, much of the charismatic world has shifted its language to center almost exclusively on "Holy Spirit." Conferences are themed around Him, worship songs call to Him, prayers are directed to Him, and while Scripture affirms the reality and power of the Spirit, we must be careful not to separate the Spirit from the Son.

The Holy Spirit does not come to replace Jesus or compete for attention. He comes to reveal Him.

"When the Counselor comes... he will testify about me." — John 15:26
"He will glorify me, because he will take from what is mine and declare it to you." — John 16:14
"no one can say, "Jesus is Lord," except by the Holy Spirit." — 1 Corinthians 12:3

The Spirit is not a vibe or a mystical substitute for Jesus. He is the Spirit of Christ (Romans 8:9; Galatians 4:6; Philippians 1:19). His work is to draw us deeper into the life, teaching, and reign of Christ. If our experiences with the Spirit aren't leading us to love Jesus more, walk in His truth more, and bear His character more, then we might be experiencing something spiritual, but it's not His Kingdom.

The Spirit glorifies Jesus and empowers us to follow Him. He makes Jesus real, personal, and present. But He never takes center stage.

Jesus is the Word made flesh.
Jesus is the Lamb slain before the foundation of the world.
Jesus is the One seated on the throne.
Jesus is the One to whom every knee will bow.

The Spirit is holy. He is God. He is precious and powerful. But He did not die for you. Jesus did.

With a proper perspective of Christ, the Spirit doesn't diminish. He delights in shining the spotlight on Jesus. That's how we know it's truly Him.

So don't settle for vague "spiritual" vibes. Be Christ-focused. Let the Spirit do what He was sent to do: awaken your heart to the glory of Jesus.

Christ in You: The Mystery and the Power

One of the most glorious and mysterious truths of the gospel is this: Jesus doesn't just save you. He comes to dwell in you.

"Christ in you, the hope of glory." — Colossians 1:27
"I no longer live, but Christ lives in me...." — Galatians 2:20
"Remain in me, and I in you..." — John 15:4

This is not motivational theology — it's supernatural reality.

We are not following Jesus at a distance, trying to live like Him. He lives in us. Through the Spirit, His very life becomes our source. His thoughts renew our mind, His power strengthens our walk, and His love flows through our heart.

Christ-centered living isn't just about putting Jesus first in your list of priorities. It's about recognizing that He is the list. He's not one part of your life — He *is* your life.

"When Christ, who is your life, appears..." — Colossians 3:4

We don't just live *for* Christ. We live *from* Christ.

What Christ-Centered Living Looks Like

Living with Jesus at the center doesn't just change how we feel, it changes how we live. It reshapes everything from identity to decisions, thoughts to desires. When Christ becomes the center, He stops being part of our life and becomes the source of it.

Here's what that kind of living looks like:

He Defines Your Identity

You are not the sum of your mistakes.
You are not what others have said about you.
You are not your trauma, your success, your title, or your history.

In Christ, your identity is no longer based on performance—it's based on position. You are in Him. You are a new creation (2 Corinthians 5:17). Chosen. Adopted. Accepted (Ephesians 1:4–5).

To live Christ-centered is to let His Word speak louder than your past, your emotions, or your inner critic.

Identity in Christ means you start from acceptance, not striving. You don't work for love—you work from it.

He Shapes Your Thinking

Romans 12:2 tells us to be "transformed by the renewing of your mind." That begins by dethroning self and allowing Jesus to reshape how we think about God, ourselves, others, and life itself.

Philippians 2:5 (ESV) urges us to "have this mind among yourselves, which is yours in Christ Jesus." The mindset of Jesus that is humble, obedient, servant-hearted is not natural, but it becomes possible when He is central.

Christ-centered thinking refuses to obsess over self, success, or survival. It thinks in terms of eternity, purpose, and surrender.

This is more than positive thinking; it's Kingdom perspective where you start seeing things differently. You begin to see conflict as an opportunity, trials as training, people as image-bearers, and life as mission.

He Leads Your Decisions

In a self-led life, the question is always, "What do *I* want to do?"
But in a Christ-centered life, the question shifts to, "What honors the King?"

Proverbs 3:6 says, *"In all your ways acknowledge Him, and He will make your paths straight."* Colossians 3:17 calls us to do everything *"in the name of the Lord Jesus."*

This doesn't mean we pray about what cereal to buy. It means that Jesus gets the final say in our direction, our relationships, our finances, and our opportunities.

We no longer move based on fear or ego, but on His voice and His peace.

A Christ-centered life doesn't just ask, "Is this allowed?"
It asks, "Is this aligned with His heart?"

He Governs Your Desires

Psalm 37:4 says, *take delight in the Lord, and he will give you your heart's desires.*" This isn't about using God to get what you want; it's about wanting what He gives.

As you spend time with Jesus, your appetite changes. You begin to long for what He loves. You grieve what grieves Him. You celebrate what brings Him joy.

Desires like comfort, control, and recognition start to lose their grip, while desires like humility, purity, generosity, and truth start to rise in you.

In Christ-centered living, your deepest wants begin to reflect Heaven's will.

He Becomes Your Ultimate Goal

When Jesus is central, life isn't reaching a destination like heaven; it's about abiding in His presence.
Success fades, titles change, and seasons shift, but knowing Christ becomes the pursuit that outlasts all others.

Paul put it plainly in Philippians 3:10 (NIV): *"I want to know Christ—yes, to know the power of His resurrection and participation in His sufferings, becoming like Him in His death"*

Not just knowing about Jesus.
Not just quoting Him.
Knowing Him.

To be Christ-centered is to make Him the treasure, not the ticket.
The aim, not the assistant.
The King, not the consultant.

A Christ-centered life doesn't ask, "How can Jesus help me reach my goals?" It says, "Jesus, You *are* the goal."

Common Substitutes for Jesus at the Center

It's not always sin that displaces Jesus from the center — sometimes it's "good" things that quietly take His place.

Here are some of the most common spiritual substitutes:

Church Culture – It's possible to love your church's style, vibe, or tradition more than Jesus Himself.

Ministry Success – Serving God can become your identity, even when intimacy with Him is missing.

Spiritual Experiences – We chase the next emotional high rather than anchoring ourselves in the unchanging presence of Christ.

Doctrinal Precision – Knowing the right truths about Jesus isn't the same as knowing Jesus.

Political Ideology – When your allegiance to a cause or party shapes your faith more than the teachings of Christ, the center has shifted.

These substitutes aren't always obvious, and that's what makes them dangerous.

Sometimes, we're worshiping our idea of Jesus rather than Jesus Himself. We've built a faith that's functional, even impressive — but hollow at the center.

The call to Christ-centered living is a call to burn away everything that competes for His throne.

Self-Centered Christianity vs. Christ-Centered Life

Often the biggest obstacle to living Christ-Centered is being self-centered. This has ultimately been mankind's problem since the very beginning. Sometimes the most subtle version of self-centeredness is a Christianity that still revolves around *you*.

Here's how the contrast plays out:

Self-Centered Faith	Christ-Centered Life
"Jesus, help me live my dream."	"Jesus, I surrender to You."
"How can You bless my plans?"	"What's on Your heart, Lord?"
Jesus as inspiration	Jesus as King and Lord
Seeking convenience	Embracing surrender
Christianity as a belief system	Christianity as union with a Person
Adding Jesus to your story	Laying down your story for His

In self-centered faith, Jesus is your assistant, there to improve your life.

In Christ-centered living, Jesus *is* your life.

Story: From Stage to Simplicity

A close friend of mine was pastoring a large, influential church. The kind of place with multiple services, a polished team, big events, and a strong public presence. From the outside, it was thriving. But behind the scenes, he was drowning in calendars, meetings, promotions, budget planning, and personnel management. He told me:

"One day I looked at my week and realized, I'm managing a religious business. And somewhere along the way... Jesus got lost."

My friend wasn't angry. He wasn't burned out in the traditional sense. But he was heartbroken. The very thing he had once given his life to—helping people follow Jesus—had become a machine. A good one. A well-oiled one. But a machine nonetheless.

Eventually, he and his wife did something few would expect:
They resigned and simply walked away from it all.

They left the stage, the staff meetings, the schedule, and they joined a small, loosely gathered community of Jesus-followers meeting in homes to share meals, worship simply, and disciple one another through everyday life.

I asked him if it was difficult to let go of the structure and momentum of what he had built. He was honest in his response:

"There are parts of the traditional church model we miss. We miss the music and the sense of celebration when a large group of people gather. But what we've found here is real. Jesus is here. Not just in theory—in presence."

He told me he had never been more fruitful: leading people to Christ, walking closely with families, watching real transformation unfold in living rooms and over dinner tables.

His wife described the shift in their lives this way:

"We used to spend our lives preparing people to meet with Jesus on Sundays. Now we wake up and walk with Him every day."

That's Christ-centered living.

Christ at the Center of Everything

Jesus shouldn't just be the center of your personal faith. He must be the center of *everything*. He's not just central to salvation, but also central to creation, history, and eternity.

"All things were created through Him and for Him." — Colossians 1:16
"by Him all things hold together." — Colossians 1:17
"At the name of Jesus every knee will bow..." — Philippians 2:10–11
"From Him and through Him and to Him are all things." — Romans 11:36

The universe was spoken into existence through Him.
World history was split in half because of Him.
Every throne, every power, every knee will one day bow before Him.

So, when you place Jesus at the center of your life, you're not doing something radical, you're doing something *right*.

Christ at the center of our lives isn't just personal preference. It's God's design and our true calling. It's what we were created for!

Living From the Life Within

This is the heartbeat of Kingdom life: Christ in you, not as a distant idea but as a present reality. The Gospel was never about inviting God to orbit around your story. It is about being drawn into His. It is not about mustering up strength to imitate Him from a distance but about participating in His very life within you. The Christian life was never meant to be a checklist of outward behaviors. It is the outflow of an inward union.

When you said yes to Jesus, you did not just receive forgiveness. You received fullness. The same Spirit that raised Him from the dead now lives and breathes inside you. The same love that moved Him to the cross now pulses through your veins. The same authority that stilled storms and cast out darkness now resides within your spirit. You are not an empty vessel trying to become like Christ. You are a living temple in which Christ dwells and expresses Himself through you.

This is the miracle and the mystery of the Kingdom. We do not live for Him; we live from Him. Our identity is no longer built on what we do, but on what He has already done. Our transformation is no longer the product of self-effort but the fruit of His abiding presence. As we learn to yield, to trust, and to abide, His life begins to flow through ours, shaping our desires, renewing our minds, and empowering our actions.

Learning to live this way is not something that happens overnight. It is the journey of a lifetime. Every season, every circumstance, every challenge becomes a classroom where the Spirit teaches us how to depend on the indwelling Christ. Day by day we grow in awareness of His presence. Step by step we learn to listen for His voice. Little by little we stop striving to manage life on our own and start learning to let His life lead ours. This is discipleship at its deepest level: not external conformity, but internal transformation as Christ lives His life through us.

And this is where true freedom is found. We are no longer striving to be enough because we live from the One who is enough. We are no longer chasing approval because we live from perfect acceptance. We are no longer trying to reach heaven because heaven has taken up residence within us. This is the life Jesus died to give you, not a borrowed existence but His very own life pulsing within you.

So let this be the foundation of everything that follows. Christ is not just your example; He is your source. He is not just the goal of your journey; He is the life that carries you there. And when you learn to live from that life, from the inside out, you will discover that the Kingdom is not somewhere you go. It is Someone you carry.

Christ-Centered Living

Living This Out

Here are three simple but radical ways to make Christ the center today:

1. ***Begin and End With Jesus***
   → *Before the phone, the news, or the noise—start with Jesus.*
   → *At day's end, return to His presence.*
   (Psalm 5:3, Mark 1:35)

2. ***Ask the Right Question***
   → *"If Jesus were Lord of this moment, how would I live?"*
   Ask it in traffic. In conflict. In your finances. In your rest.

3. ***Practice His Presence in the Mundane***
   → *Whether folding laundry or grocery shopping, invite Him in.*
   Every ordinary moment becomes sacred when you see Him in it.

Reflection Questions

1. Is there any area of your life where Jesus is acknowledged but not obeyed?

2. What "good" things might be crowding out the centrality of Christ?

3. What would change in your day to day if you lived as if Jesus truly is King?

A Prayer for Re-Centering

Jesus,
I don't want to live with You on the outskirts of my life.
I want You at the center—of my thoughts, time, choices, and desires.
Strip away the noise, the clutter, and the counterfeit comforts.
Be my treasure. Be my vision. Be my King.
I surrender again—not to try harder, but to trust deeper.
Reign in me. Lead me. Be magnified in every breath.
Amen.

When Jesus becomes the center, everything else starts to shift. But one of the biggest obstacles to Kingdom living is the religious mindset we've inherited. If we're serious about following the King, we must leave behind the system that tries to control Him.

Chapter 2: Kingdom Over Religion

Allegiance to God's Kingdom—not man-made religion

"But seek first the Kingdom of God and His righteousness..." — Matthew 6:33

"These people honor me with their lips, but their hearts are far from me... their teachings are merely human rules." — Matthew 15:8–9 (NIV)

"For he has rescued us from the dominion of darkness and brought us into the kingdom of the Son he loves" — Colossians 1:13

When Religion Replaces Relationship

Let's be very clear: religion — in all its forms — is not the Kingdom. It never has been, and it never will be. No matter how polished, traditional, modern, or well-intended, religion cannot access the life of God's Kingdom. As Scripture says, it has *a form of godliness but denies its power* (2 Timothy 3:5). Religion is always a watered-down, humanized replacement for the real thing, a substitute for the actual rule and reign of God. It mimics the motions, borrows the language, and decorates the exterior, but it lacks the life, presence, and authority of the King. You can have structure without surrender and crowds without Christ. But the Kingdom? The Kingdom is not built on behavior modification or performance; it's built on the indwelling presence of Jesus and absolute allegiance to Him. This distinction matters more than we think.

Religion is a façade—a false door that doesn't lead to Kingdom life. It centers on control instead of Christ, ritual instead of relationship, tradition instead of transformation. In doing so, it becomes the very thing Jesus came to confront.

"Woe to you, teachers of the law and Pharisees, you hypocrites! You shut the door of the Kingdom of heaven in people's faces." — Matthew 23:13

Jesus didn't die to start a new belief system. He came to introduce a Kingdom, one not built on man's performance but on God's presence.

He didn't say, "Come follow rules."
He said, "Come, follow Me."

The cross wasn't the climax of a new religion. It was the doorway into a new reality; one ruled by love, not law; by presence, not performance.

My Personal Shift

For years, I lived in the world of church leadership where metrics measured success and Sunday performance was far more important than weekday devotion. We pursued the holy trinity of church growth: numbers, noise, and nickels!

Maybe we didn't intend to reduce the Kingdom to a calendar of events, but it happened quietly, slowly, subtly.

The programs became polished. The teaching was solid. But I began to feel it: something vital was missing. We were well-managed, but where was the Spirit?

We had order, but no fire. Attendance, but not allegiance. We had become a highly functioning machine, but it wasn't producing the kind of fruit Jesus described.

That's when I realized:

We had become experts at managing church, but we were missing the Kingdom; and the Kingdom cannot be managed, it must be received.

What's the Difference?

Religion says: Attend. Behave. Conform.
The Kingdom says: Abide. Believe. Be transformed.

Religion keeps people bound to systems.
The Kingdom sets people free.

Religion tries to climb up to God.
The Kingdom is God coming down to us in Christ, by His Spirit.

Religion builds walls.
The Kingdom builds tables.

Religion appeals to the flesh. It gives us a checklist, a system to master, and a sense of control, but the Kingdom demands surrender.

It doesn't invite you to manage your life better. It invites you to *lay your life down*.

Religion vs. Kingdom

Religion	Kingdom
Rule-focused	Relationship-focused
Behavior modification	Heart transformation
External appearance	Internal renewal
Driven by guilt or duty	Motivated by love and delight
Do more, try harder	Abide and be transformed
Cling to tradition and structure	Respond to the Spirit and truth
Attendance = faithfulness	Allegiance = surrender
Build systems and separation	Build family and connection
Strive for approval	Live from identity in Christ

Religion	Kingdom
Seek control	Surrender control
Measures by activity	Measures by fruit (Gal. 5:22–23)
Creates pride or shame	Cultivates humility and joy
Produces burnout or performance	Produces rest and renewal
Centers on man's efforts	Centers on Christ's rule

From Ritual to Reality

Religion is not confined to stained glass windows, incense, and scripted liturgies. Man-made ideas have infiltrated nearly every stream of Christianity from Pentecostal to Charismatic, Baptist to Lutheran, Eastern Orthodox to Evangelical, and everything in between. Whether it's performance-driven worship, celebrity pastors, denominational hierarchies, or unbiblical traditions passed down without question, the fingerprints of human invention are everywhere. The danger isn't in liturgy itself, but in substituting human systems for Kingdom reality. This bears repeating. Jesus didn't come to establish a better religion; He came to establish a Kingdom. A Kingdom that liberates us from the traps of performance, pride, and pretense.

Kingdom Values vs. Religious Traditions

It's often said that religion is man reaching for God, but the Kingdom is God coming to man. One is built on human effort, the other on divine initiative. Religion often creates structure without Spirit, systems without surrender, and hierarchy without humility. The Kingdom carries a radically different set of values. The values of heaven.

Jesus Confronted Religion Constantly

If you want to know what made Jesus angry, read the Gospels.
It wasn't the broken, the immoral, or the outcast who drew His rebuke.
It was the religious.

He flipped temple tables because the sacred space had been turned into a marketplace of greed (Matthew 21:12–13).
He exposed the Pharisees for obsessing over image while neglecting the heart (Matthew 23:5).
He called out their worship as hollow "honoring Me with lips, but hearts far away" (Matthew 15:8–9).
He said, "You nullify the Word of God for the sake of your tradition" (Matthew 15:6).

Jesus didn't come to reform the religious system. He came to replace it with Himself.

"Destroy this temple, and I will raise it up in three days." — John 2:19

He wasn't talking about a building. He was talking about His body, His presence, and His Kingdom.

Jesus' Warnings About Religion

Jesus was tender with sinners but fierce with the religious. He never yelled at a prostitute or condemned a tax collector, but He did call religious leaders "whitewashed tombs" and "blind guides" (Matthew 23:27, 24). Why? Because religion can blind people to their need for grace.

In Matthew 23, Jesus delivers a scathing rebuke to the scribes and Pharisees. He exposes the damage of a religious system that looks holy on the outside but is full of pride and self-righteousness on the inside.

"They tie up heavy loads that are hard to carry and put them on people's shoulders, but they themselves aren't willing to lift a finger to move them."— Matthew 23:4

This is what religion does. It piles on expectations and demands, without offering power or freedom. It creates insiders and outsiders. It teaches people to perform instead of transform. Worst of all, it uses God's name to do it.

Jesus came to lift burdens, not add to them. He came to break chains, not create more rules.

If the way you're practicing your faith leads to fear, shame, exhaustion, or pride, then it's time to ask: is this the Kingdom, or is this religion?

Religion as Part of the World System

We often assume religion is holy by default. It isn't. Religion is one of the greatest enemies of the Kingdom. Why? Because it gives people just enough God to stay unchanged. It mimics holiness but resists surrender. It protects power, resists truth, and often partners with the very systems Jesus came to upend.

Religion is not just a distraction; it is part of the world system.
Just like politics, money, and entertainment, it can be used to control people, build platforms, and suppress truth.
That's why Paul warned the Colossians to beware of "philosophy and empty deceit, based on human tradition and the elemental forces of the world" (Colossians 2:8).

The religious spirit is not neutral. It is anti-Kingdom. It wears spiritual clothing but denies the King's rule. It can quote Scripture while crucifying the Savior.

This is why Jesus' strongest words were never for sinners; they were for the self-righteous. The Pharisees weren't just misguided; they were functioning as gatekeepers against grace. They upheld tradition while rejecting truth in the flesh. They clung to their system and missed the Savior.

Story: The Elder, the Hat, and What He Missed

David had been an elder at his church for over two decades. He was devoted, disciplined, and deeply respected. He made sure the sanctuary was clean, the theology was sound, and the traditions were honored. To him, reverence for God meant order, excellence, and a certain kind of dignity, especially on the platform.

One Sunday morning, David sat in his usual seat near the front, scanning the worship team. That's when he saw it: a young man—barely twenty—standing on stage with a ball cap on his head and ripped jeans at the knees, leading worship like he belonged there. David's jaw tightened. *"Where is the respect?"* he thought.

The service went on, but David was too distracted to hear the message. His spirit was grieved not because of heresy, but because of a hat.

What he missed was the miracle.

That very morning, four people gave their lives to Jesus—including the husband of a long-time church member. A man the church had prayed for faithfully for nearly twenty years. That morning, he stood with tears in his eyes, hands lifted, finally saying yes to the King.

But David couldn't see it. His eyes weren't on the altar; they were on the platform. He left the service fuming, not rejoicing.

By the next week, he had scheduled a meeting with the board.
"I believe the pastor is compromising," he said. "He's letting just anyone on the stage. There are no standards, no reverence. I'm calling for a vote of no confidence."

No one spoke for a moment. Then one board member quietly asked, "David, what did you think of the salvations last week?"

David paused. He hadn't even heard about them.

Religious loyalty will guard the platform while ignoring the altar.
It will protect the rules and miss the resurrection. It will fight for order, even as people are being reborn right in front of it.

Jesus isn't offended by hats, but He is grieved when hearts care more about appearances than transformation.

Deconstructing Religion Without Losing the King

We live in a time where many are questioning the faith they inherited. Some call it "deconstruction." Others see it as rebellion. But the truth is, many people aren't trying to walk away from Jesus, they're just trying to walk away from man-made religion *in order to find Him*.

That longing isn't wrong. In fact, it may be the Holy Spirit at work.

Jesus did not come to affirm religious systems. He came to expose and confront them. The harshest words He ever spoke were to the religious elite of His day (see Matthew 23). The early church was born *outside* the temple system. Paul spent most of his ministry confronting legalism and religious distortion.

So, if you're pulling away from institutions, traditions, or leaders that felt more about control than Christ, don't feel like you're betraying your faith. You may actually be waking up to the Kingdom.

"His voice shook the earth at that time, but now he has promised, Yet once more I will shake not only the earth but also the heavens.' ... so that what is not shaken might remain"— Hebrews 12:26–27

God is shaking man-made religion, not to destroy faith but to purify it.

Just be careful: don't throw out Jesus with the system. The religious church may appear to be broken, but the King and His Kingdom surely are not. His Church is beautiful, thriving, and filled with His life.

The system may have failed you, but the Savior never will. Let Him rebuild what religion broke.

The Kingdom Is a New Operating System

Jesus didn't come to offer a patch for Judaism or any other religion. He came to install an entirely new operating system. A new way of being, thinking, and living.

In Luke 5:37–38, Jesus says the Kingdom is like new wine that won't fit into old wineskins.

Paul echoes this in Colossians 2:20–23: warning the Church not to fall back into human rules and self-made religion, which "lack any value in restraining sensual indulgence."

Religion can polish the outside, but His Kingdom transforms the inside.

What we often call "religion" isn't neutral; it's part of the world system. It offers structure without surrender, image without intimacy, and conformity without Christ. That's why it can never lead us into the Kingdom. In fact, it often becomes one of the greatest obstacles to it.

We'll explore this more deeply later, where we'll unpack how religion, like politics, consumerism, and other things can subtly pull us away from the reign of Jesus and what it means to live truly free under His rule.

Story: From Duty to Delight

I once met a lady at a church where I was frequently asked to speak at, who was known for her perfect church attendance, knowledge of Scripture, and a spotless moral record. She looked the part. She appeared to have done everything right.

One night at the end of a revival service she came to me and told me through tears, "I don't know if I've ever really known Jesus. I know the church. I know the Bible. But I want to know *Him*."

That moment became a holy interruption. She started opening her Bible not for information, but for encounter. Her prayers shifted from polished performances to honest conversations. Little by little, joy began to ignite. The language of duty gave way to the language of delight. Religion gave way to revelation. She was no longer just attending church; she was a member of the body of Christ and a citizen of His kingdom.

Not just informed but transformed.

That's the difference. Religion demands better behavior while the Kingdom births a new heart and that contrast is huge!

Signs You Might Be Living Religious, Not Kingdom

Religion is sneaky. It can sound right, feel familiar, and even look productive. But it often keeps us busy for God while keeping us distant from Him. Here are some signs that what you're living may be more religious than Kingdom:

You serve out of guilt more than joy.
You say "yes" because you're afraid of letting others down, not because you've been with Jesus and want to love people from overflow. Serving becomes exhausting instead of life-giving.

You measure your righteousness by comparison, not by Christ.
You feel spiritual when you're doing more than others or ashamed when you're not. Your sense of worth rises and falls with performance, rather than resting in Jesus' finished work.

You focus more on appearances than transformation.
You worry about looking "put together," but avoid the inner work of surrender, healing, and heart change. The outside looks clean, but the inside feels dry.

You equate church activity with spiritual maturity.
You're constantly attending, volunteering, or producing, but you rarely pause to simply sit with Jesus. Presence has been replaced by productivity.

You feel more burdened than free.
Instead of the easy yoke Jesus promised, your faith feels like a list of never-ending expectations. Joy is rare. Rest is elusive. And grace feels like a theory, not a reality.

If any of these hits close to home don't run from it.
That's not condemnation.
It's invitation.

"Come to Me, all who are weary and burdened, and I will give you rest."
— Matthew 11:28

The Kingdom was never meant to be a proving ground. It isn't the place where you strive to become enough, perform to earn love, or climb higher in hopes of finally being accepted. It's the place where all of that striving ceases and where you stop running after identity and begin living from the one you've already been given. In the Kingdom, you don't have to manufacture purpose; you simply awaken to the purpose that's been woven into you from the beginning. You don't earn a name here; you receive one; spoken by the One who knew you before you knew yourself.

It's not about getting every step right or checking every box. The Kingdom is not a scoreboard; it's a sanctuary. It's not about achieving perfection; it's about surrendering to the Perfect One. This isn't a call to perform harder but to trust deeper and to trade the pressure of proving for the peace of abiding. When you realize that Jesus has already done everything necessary, you stop living *for* approval and start living *from* it. You stop climbing ladders to heaven and instead rest in the One who brought heaven near.

In this way, His Kingdom becomes more than a concept or idea, instead it becomes the atmosphere you breathe. You find that what God desires is not your flawless record but your yielded heart. The Kingdom is not a reward for the deserving but a refuge for the surrendered. And as you release the need to "get it right," you discover something far better: the joy of walking with the One who already has.

A Call to Allegiance

Allegiance is more than agreement.
It's not just saying "I believe in Jesus."
It's declaring, *"Jesus is my King and everything else must bow."*

You can believe the right things and still build your life around yourself.
You can attend church regularly and still be loyal to comfort, convenience, or culture.
You can sing about Jesus on Sunday and still serve a system—whether religious, political, or personal—that has nothing to do with His Kingdom.

Allegiance isn't about lip service. It's about loyalty.

"We've made Jesus too polite, too passive. But He wears a crown, not a cardigan. He rules with love, but He does rule." -Frank Viola

To choose the Kingdom is to transfer your loyalty from your preferences, your politics, and your personal goals to Jesus the King. It's not about inviting Him to bless your plans. It's about laying down your life so He can build something entirely new.

Allegiance means Jesus defines:

Your truth
Your priorities
Your values
Your decisions
Your identity
Your direction

It's the difference between admiration and submission, between agreement and surrender. Between adding Jesus to your life and losing your life to follow Him.

"If anyone wants to follow after me, let him deny himself, take up his cross daily, and follow me." — Luke 9:23

This is not harsh—it's holy.
It's not a heavy burden—it's the doorway to freedom.
It's not legalism—it's liberation under a good King.

So, the question isn't, *Do I believe in Jesus?*
The question is, *Have I bowed to Him?*

Allegiance to Jesus Over Doctrines and Denominations

One of the most deceptive forms of religion today isn't legalism. Its identity based in theological camps or denominational loyalty.

We begin to define our faith by labels: I'm Reformed. I'm Spirit-filled. I'm non-denominational. I'm *whatever*! And slowly, our allegiance shifts from the King to the camp.

But the Kingdom is not divided.

Jesus didn't come to start a denomination. He came to make disciples. He didn't die to preserve theological tribes. He died to bring us into a new family, a Kingdom of priests, where the only banner is His name.

"But everything that was a gain to me, I have considered to be a loss because of Christ."— Philippians 3:7

The apostle Paul had pedigree, education, flawless doctrine, but said it was all *worthless* compared to knowing Jesus.

This doesn't mean doctrine doesn't matter, it just means that Jesus matters more. The Kingdom is not about choosing sides. It's about choosing surrender.

Ask yourself: is my identity in a movement, or in Christ?

Living This Out

1. ***Trade Performance for Presence***
   → *Begin each day by asking, "What does it look like to walk with You today, King Jesus?"*
2. ***Question Cultural Norms***
   → *Ask, "Is this just what Christians do? Or is this what Jesus taught?"*
3. ***Break the Sunday–Monday Divide***
   → *The Kingdom isn't a weekend event. It's an every-moment reality. Practice His presence in your home, workplace, conversations, and quiet places.*

Reflection Questions

1. Where have I been living more by tradition than by truth?

2. In what ways has religion shaped or distorted my view of God?

3. What would change if my full allegiance belonged to the King and His Kingdom?

A Prayer of Allegiance

Jesus,
I lay down every man-made attempt to earn what You've already given. I renounce performance. I surrender pretense. I reject religion without relationships. I give You my full allegiance not just my belief, but my obedience. Teach me to live kingdom centered. Rewire my heart for delight, not duty. Be my King not just in word, but in truth.
Amen.

The Kingdom isn't built on platforms, it's built on people.
And it doesn't grow through performance, but through shared life.
Once we leave behind religion, we're invited into something deeper:
real community, where discipleship gets
messy, honest, and transformative.

Chapter 3: Discipleship Through Community

We grow in Christ together, not alone.

"By this everyone will know that you are my disciples, if you love one another." — *John 13:35*

"They devoted themselves to the apostles' teaching, to the fellowship, to the breaking of bread, and to prayer." — *Acts 2:42*

"not neglecting to gather together, as some are in the habit of doing, but encouraging each other..." — *Hebrews 10:25*

Discipleship Was Never Meant to Be Solo

In the Western world, we've often reduced discipleship to private devotion, quiet time, podcasts, reading plans, curriculum completion, and sermons on demand. And while those practices can nourish us, they were never designed to carry the full weight of spiritual formation. You can learn *about* Jesus in isolation, but you become *like* Jesus in community.

Real discipleship is the kind that forms us, stretches us, refines us, and matures us. And it happens primarily in the context of relationships. You can't be sharpened alone. You can't practice humility, forgiveness, patience, or love in a vacuum. Those things are formed where people are present and sometimes painfully imperfect.

Discipleship doesn't happen in isolation. It happens around tables, in living rooms, and in everyday moments where love meets accountability.

Jesus didn't start a school or a seminar. He didn't publish a manual or run a conference. He invited people into His life. He said, "Come, follow Me," (Matthew 4:19). And then He walked with them, ate with them, taught them, rebuked them, wept with them and empowered them. Together!

Even when they didn't get it.
Even when they argued.
Even when they betrayed and abandoned Him.
He stayed in relationship.

Discipleship is slow and sacred work, forged in the fires of shared life. It's less about finishing a workbook and more about walking with Jesus and with one another in grace and truth.

This is the model we see in the early Church: believers gathering daily, breaking bread, praying, confessing, serving, and growing *together* (Acts 2:42–47).

We've often misunderstood Paul's words in Ephesians 4 because we've read them through a cultural lens rather than a Kingdom one. In much of the modern Church, *apostle, prophet, evangelist, pastor,* and *teacher* have been treated as titles to be claimed, positions to be held, or ranks to be achieved almost like badges on a spiritual résumé. But Paul was never describing an ecclesiastical hierarchy; he was painting a picture of how the life of Christ is expressed through His people in different ways for the sake of the whole.

A better word than "gift" might be *gracing*, a manifestation of God's grace operating through a person to serve and strengthen the community. These aren't callings that elevate one believer above another; they're functions designed to equip, empower, and mature the Body together. An apostolic grace pioneers and establishes new ground for the Kingdom. A prophetic grace calls the Church back to God's heart and points toward His purposes. An evangelistic grace carries the Good News beyond the walls. A pastoral grace nurtures, shepherds, and walks with people. A teaching grace grounds the community in truth and understanding. None of these are titles to be worn with pride; they are responsibilities to be carried with humility.

And if we're tempted to think of these graces as special or reserved for a spiritual elite, we need only look to Jesus — the fullness of all five embodied in one life. He was the **Apostle**, sent from the Father to establish the

Kingdom on earth (Hebrews 3:1). He was the **Prophet**, declaring the heart and will of God and calling people back to the truth. He was the **Evangelist**, proclaiming the Good News of the Kingdom and inviting all who would hear to enter in. He was the **Pastor**, the Good Shepherd who knew His sheep by name and laid down His life for them. And He was the **Teacher**, revealing the mysteries of God and opening the Scriptures so that hearts could burn with understanding.

But here's the stunning truth: Jesus never intended to keep these expressions of grace to Himself. Instead, He shared His own life with us. Not just forgiveness, but *function*. Not just redemption, but *responsibility*. Through the Spirit, He now distributes these same graces among His people so that His ministry might continue through His Body on the earth. What He was in fullness, we now reflect in part, each of us carrying a measure of His nature so that together we might reveal His whole.

This is the beauty and mystery of the Church. The goal was never for a few individuals to imitate Jesus from a distance but for a whole people to embody His life together. The apostolic grace pioneers because Christ still builds. The prophetic grace speaks because Christ still calls. The evangelistic grace reaches because Christ still seeks the lost. The pastoral grace shepherds because Christ still cares. The teaching grace instructs because Christ still reveals truth. And as each part does its work, the whole Body "grows and builds itself up in love" (Ephesians 4:16), until we no longer just talk about Jesus. We *collectively look like Him*.

"From him the whole body, fitted and knit together by every supporting ligament, promotes the growth of the body for building itself up in love by the proper working of each individual part." (Ephesians 4:16).

You need the Body and the Body needs you.

Maturity doesn't come from isolation. It comes from interdependence when we speak the truth in love, carry one another's burdens, forgive freely, and serve with joy. This is how we grow up into Christ, our Head.

If our version of discipleship never costs us comfort, never invites us into vulnerability, never forces us to forgive or be forgiven, it may be information but it's not transformation.

We were never meant to grow alone.

The Early Church Was a Family, Not an Event

Acts 2:42–47 paints a radically different picture than most modern church experiences. The early believers didn't just attend something once or even twice a week; they shared their lives.

They ate together
Prayed together
Studied together
Worshiped together
Met each other's needs together
Carried one another's burdens together
Practiced generosity, confession, and mutual growth together

This wasn't a spiritual hobby. It was a Kingdom family.
It wasn't just to gather, it was *together*!!

My Turning Point

For a long time, I believed that discipleship primarily happened from the stage. I thought if I taught well, preached with passion, and pointed people to Scripture, they would naturally grow. I was convinced that inspired preaching and revelatory teaching would produce transformation. I assumed that if I shared enough of the truth I carried, it would change their lives.

But over time, I noticed something unsettling: my best efforts weren't producing transformation. People could quote theology but didn't love their neighbor. They could fill notebooks with sermon notes, but their marriages were still falling apart. They were faithful on Sunday but isolated and often wavering the rest of the week.

Then came a moment that shifted everything.

I was invited into a simple Bible study group. No platform. No lights. No stage or structured program. Just a small room full of people trying to find Jesus, sharing a meal, opening the Word, praying for each other, and having real conversations about real life.

There was laughter. There were tears. There was honesty and hunger.

And in that small setting, I saw more spiritual growth, more vulnerability, and more hunger for Christ in just a few months than I had seen in several years of evangelistic endeavors, revival meetings, and big events.

That night and the many that followed convinced me of something I can't unsee:
Discipleship isn't a presentation. It's participation.
It grows where people are seen, known, and challenged in love.
It grows in community. It grows where life is shared.

Here is where heaven touches earth and where the Kingdom becomes more than words.

Why We Avoid It

Let's be honest: community is messy.

It's easier to just watch online, attend church, or listen to a podcast than to open our hearts to real people. When we stay on the sidelines, we avoid the risk of being misunderstood. We don't have to deal with offense, conflict, or correction. We fear rejection. We resist accountability. We worry that if people really knew us, they might not accept us. So, we settle for content instead of connection.

But the Kingdom doesn't grow in isolation. It grows in the context of community, not in sanitized rows, but around messy tables, shared burdens, and mutual grace. This is the soil where God grows us.

You'll never be fully formed in Christ apart from His Body.
He didn't save you to give you a spot at the table, He placed you into a family.

We avoid community because it costs us something, usually our comfort, convenience, and control.

It forces us out of hiding. It confronts our selfishness. It stretches our patience. In true community, you can't curate your image or control the narrative. People see the real you—flaws, fears, and all. And that's exactly where transformation begins.

Comfort says, *"Keep it surface-level."*
Convenience says, *"Engage when it's easy."*
Control says, *"Stay in charge of your image."*
But the Kingdom says, *"Lay it all down. Be known. Be loved. Be sharpened."*

Real discipleship demands presence and presence requires surrender.
That's why true Kingdom community isn't built on preference but in partnership.

And the reward is far greater: transformation, healing, and a love that not only looks like Jesus, the kind of love that flourishes where *"two or three are gathered together in My name"* and where *He Himself is present in the midst of them* (Matthew 18:20).

Close Enough to Grow

I remember when my wife and I were pastoring our first church. A pastor's wife we deeply respected, someone seasoned by years in ministry pulled us aside and offered what she believed was wisdom:

"Don't ever get too close to the people in your church. Love them at a distance. If you let people in too far, they'll hurt you."

She wasn't bitter, maybe just bruised. And in a way, she was right.

But we didn't take her advice.

We opened our hearts, our home, and our lives to the people we were shepherding. We prayed with them, ate with them, grieved with them, celebrated with them. We let people in not just to the front porch of our lives, but all the way to the kitchen table.

And yes, we got hurt.

We were betrayed by people we had trusted.
Lied about by people we had defended.
Taken advantage of by people we had sacrificed for.

We got hurt. A lot.

But here's the truth: Jesus met us in that pain and the very openness that allowed the wounding also made space for deep healing. Our hurt didn't harden us, it humbled us and strangely somehow, it grew us. We learned to forgive from the inside out. We learned that real love doesn't keep people at arm's length.

We have never regretted letting people get close. Because ministry isn't performance, it's presence. And presence always carries risk.

But it also carries the possibility. The possibility of resurrection, of love stronger than fear, and of connection deeper than wounds.

This is discipleship. Not polished programs, but shared lives. Not curated curriculum, but mutual care. Discipleship happens at eye level, in community where vulnerability is welcome and transformation is possible. You can't microwave maturity, and you can't program deep formation. It happens in the grit and grace of walking together, wounds and all.

Remember Jesus didn't train His disciples from a distance. He walked with them, ate with them, and wept with them. He let them in close even when He knew it would hurt.

And if we're going to follow Him, we must be willing to do the same.

The Messy Beauty of Real Discipleship

Discipleship isn't just a curriculum to be followed, though a little structure can be helpful. But let's be honest: Jesus didn't hand His disciples a PDF or a manual. He shared life with them. He corrected them and called them higher. It didn't take twelve weeks or twelve steps, it took their whole lives.

We've often reduced discipleship to a pre-packaged class, a four-step growth track, or a Dream Team onboarding sequence, as if Kingdom transformation could be scheduled and systematized. Spiritual formation isn't factory work. You can't mass-produce maturity.

That's why years of church membership and faithful attendance haven't produced an army of disciples. We've filled seats but neglected lives. We've built congregations but not communities of Christ-followers. Attendance doesn't equal transformation, not unless people are invited into real relationships that sharpen, stretch, and shape them into the image of Jesus.

True discipleship is gritty and relational. It's inconvenient. It disrupts our calendars and challenges our comfort zones. It happens in the ordinary moments in living rooms, over coffee, in text messages and tears, through rebuke and encouragement, grace and truth.

When Scripture says, "As iron sharpens iron, so one person sharpens another" (Proverbs 27:17), it's not describing a cozy Bible study. Iron sharpening iron involves friction, sparks, and pressure. It's noisy. It's messy. It's uncomfortable. But that's what makes it powerful.

In that mess, dull lives are shaped into sharp instruments for the glory of the King.

What Kingdom Community Looks Like

It's Relational, Not Transactional

You're not a consumer. You're a participant. Kingdom community isn't built on convenience, programs, or personalities. It's rooted in *relationship*. You're not a customer showing up for a service—you're a vital part of the Body. Your presence matters. Your voice matters. You're not a spectator in the stands; you're a participant in the game.
(*Romans 12:4–5, 1 Corinthians 12:12–27*)

It's Honest, Not Performative

There's no pressure to fake it. Confession and vulnerability are welcomed, not punished. You don't have to pretend in the Kingdom. You're not expected to wear a mask or polish your image. In true community, weakness is not a liability, it's an invitation. Vulnerability becomes the doorway to healing, and confession creates space for connection
(*James 5:16, Galatians 6:1–2*)

It's Formational, Not Comfortable

Community will challenge your ego, expose blind spots, and teach you how to love like Jesus. Real community isn't always easy. It will rub against your preferences, challenge your pride, and expose areas where love has yet to grow. But this is where transformation happens. Friction isn't failure, it's formation. We are sharpened and shaped into the likeness of Christ *together*. (*Proverbs 27:17, Ephesians 4:15–16*)

It's Purposeful, Not Passive

Every member is vital. You have something to give, and something to receive. In the Kingdom, no one is insignificant. Every person carries a piece of the puzzle. You weren't designed to just show up, you're called to show up *with purpose and on purpose*. You have something to offer that someone else needs and you need something that someone else carries. The Spirit has distributed gifts intentionally and your role matters. (*1 Peter 4:10, Romans 12:6–8*)

Story: From BBQ to Breakthrough

His name was Robert. A tough, quiet former Marine with a thousand-yard stare and no interest in church. He wasn't hostile, just hardened. Years of military service, childhood wounds, and life's disappointments had built a thick shell around his heart. Faith? That was his wife's thing.

She had started attending church regularly and joined a women's Bible study. She was growing, healing, changing—and she wanted Robert to experience what she had found. So, with a little coaxing and a lot of eye-rolling, Robert agreed to go to church with her. Not because he was drawn to it, but because it made her happy.

He came. Sat stiffly through services. Arms folded. Expression unreadable. He never sang. Never smiled. But he showed up.

Then something simple and profound happened.

A few of the men from the church invited Robert to a backyard BBQ one night while the women were having a fellowship night. It wasn't a Bible study. No altar call. Just burgers, laughter, and conversation around a fire pit. Robert came and, to his own surprise, he enjoyed it. The guys didn't pressure him; they just included him.

That pattern continued with BBQs, ballgames, firepits, and workdays. Over time, the shell began to crack. Robert started opening up. Sharing stories from his past—some of them raw and painful. Childhood scars. Combat trauma. The kind of things he never thought he'd say out loud.

Robert shared, "I don't even know when it happened. There wasn't a lightning strike or an altar call. But somewhere along the way, I realized I had changed. I was praying. I was trusting Jesus and my heart was tender and full."

Robert became a pillar in that church. On Sundays, you would see him at the front of the church, hands lifted, tears flowing, worshiping the Jesus who transformed him. Not into someone else, but into who he was always meant to be a gentle giant, full of grace and compassion.

During the week you'd find Robert mentoring young men, sharing his story, and pointing them to Christ, not with polished words, but with a life that proved discipleship works best around tables, firepits, and friendships.

Don't Blame the Church

It's easy to blame the church. To point at its failures, flaws, and hypocrisies and conclude, *"That's why I don't go anymore."* But when we talk about the Church—the true ekklesia of Christ—we're not talking about a building, a brand, or a broken institution. We're talking about the Body of Christ.

Ekklesia is the greek New Testament term meaning "called-out ones," often translated as "church." Originally used to describe a gathering of citizens in ancient Greek culture, Jesus redefined *ekklesia* to mean the community of those called out of the world to live under His Kingship. It's not about a building or institution, but a people who embody the values and mission of God's Kingdom.

Yes, man-made versions of church often fall short. Religion wrapped in performance and consumerism leaves people empty, but don't confuse the counterfeit with the real.

The **ekklesia**—the called-out assembly of God's people—isn't broken down. It's not a failed idea. It's *His* idea. In fact, Scripture gives us several powerful images of what the Church truly is:

The Body of Christ – 1 Corinthians 12:27

The Bride of Christ – Ephesians 5:25–27

The Household of God – Ephesians 2:19

The Temple of the Holy Spirit – 1 Corinthians 3:16–17

A Holy Nation and Royal Priesthood – 1 Peter 2:9

The Pillar and Support of the Truth – 1 Timothy 3:15

God's Field / God's Building – 1 Corinthians 3:9

A Spiritual House of Living Stones – 1 Peter 2:5

The Assembly of the Firstborn – Hebrews 12:23

The Flock of God – 1 Peter 5:2

The Church of the Firstborn – Hebrews 12:23

The Vine and the Branches – John 15:5

A People for His Own Possession – 1 Peter 2:9

The **ekklesia** is not man's idea; it's God's answer. It's the visible expression of His invisible Kingdom on earth.

It's messy because people are messy. But it's also glorious because Christ is the Head, and we are His Body. You were never meant to follow Jesus alone. The Kingdom is not a solo mission. It's a family, a fellowship, a body, a bride.

To reject the Church is to reject part of God's design for your transformation and mission. The Church *is* the Kingdom in community. Not perfect, but being perfected and not optional, but essential.

So don't walk away from the church (ekklesia). Lean in. Connect. Commit.

The Church is Christ's answer for His community.

It is His Kingdom on earth.

How We Grow Together

Jesus said the world would recognize His disciples not by our theology degrees, our Instagram posts, or our perfect doctrine, but by our love (John 13:35).
Not casual love or polished love. Not convenient love, but real love; the kind that costs you something.

And that kind of love isn't microwaved. It's marinated over time.
Forged in commitment, seasoned with patience, and then refined through humility and held together by grace.

You can't mass-produce spiritual maturity.
You can't fake genuine friendship.
And you can't outsource discipleship to a class or a pastor.

Discipleship through community isn't a program. It's a lifestyle.
It's a long walk in the same direction, side by side under the rule of the King.

It's sitting together in joy and sorrow, confessing sin and celebrating victories.

It's lovingly correcting one another when we stray and embracing each other when we return.

It's praying together, weeping together, and sometimes wrestling through Scripture together.

It's asking hard questions and refusing to give easy answers.

In community, we learn how to be the Church, not just attend one.
We begin to see discipleship not as a checkbox on a form, but as a shared journey of transformation.

We grow because we are known.
We grow because we are challenged.
We grow because the Spirit moves through the Body, not just the pulpit.

This is the Kingdom way: not lone wolves, but linked arms.
Not performance, but participation.
Not shallow connection, but sacrificial love.

That's how we grow. Together.

Restored on the Shoreline

We see this beautifully in the life of Peter. He was bold, passionate, and fiercely loyal—quick to speak and quicker to act. He was the first to declare, "You are the Christ, the Son of the living God" (Matthew 16:16). He swore he would never abandon Jesus (Matthew 26:33).

And yet, in Jesus' darkest hour, Peter denied Him three times (Luke 22:54–62).

Ashamed and disillusioned, he didn't just fail—he fled. He returned to his old life, back to fishing, empty and broken (John 21:3).

But then Jesus came. The risen Christ met Peter on that same shoreline, not with rebuke, but with breakfast. The fish were already caught and cooked. Peter brought nothing, yet Jesus had provided everything (John 21:9).

In that moment, Jesus restored him.
Not by giving him a platform, but by reminding him of his purpose: "Do you love Me? Then feed My sheep." (John 21:15–17)

Discipleship isn't about perfection—it's about presence.
It's about receiving grace and returning to the purpose Jesus always had for us: To love Him and to love one another.

Living This Out

1. Join or Start a Kingdom-Minded Group

→ *Don't wait for someone else to organize it. Invite a few hungry believers. Open your home. Share a meal. Open the Word. Pray together.*

2. Be Known

→ *Take off the mask. Let someone see the real you. Share your joy and, possibly your pain. Discipleship requires transparency.*

3. Invest in Others

→ *Who can you walk with? Who are you encouraging, mentoring, or calling higher in love?*

Reflection Questions

1. Are you walking in true spiritual community or settling for Christian acquaintances?

2.   What's holding you back from deeper connection and accountability?

3.   What could happen in your life if you were fully known and fully loved in the Body of Christ?

A Prayer for Kingdom Relationships

Jesus,

Thank You for placing me in Your Body. Forgive me for trying to follow You alone. Teach me to value community as You do. Give me the humility to be known, the courage to love deeply, and the faith to walk with others in grace and truth. Use my life to build others and use them to form me.

Amen.

Community shapes us, but so does culture.
And if we're not careful, the values of the world can start discipling us more than the ways of Jesus.
Let's talk about what it really means to live free from the gravitational pull of the world's system.

Chapter 4: Freedom from the World System

Live in the world—without being shaped by it.

"Do not conform to the pattern of this world but be transformed by the renewing of your mind." — *Romans 12:2 (ESV)*

"My Kingdom is not of this world..." — *John 18:36*

"Come out from among them and be separate, says the Lord." — *2 Corinthians 6:17*

More Than Forgiveness—Freedom

Many believers accept Jesus for the forgiveness of sin, but few step into the freedom of His Kingdom. Why? Because we've been discipled by the world's system more than the Word of God. Even after salvation, many still live by the world's rhythms, values, and assumptions.

But Jesus didn't come just to save us *from* sin. He came to call us *out* of a system. Jesus didn't just die to take you to Heaven. He died to get Heaven into you, so you could live free from the world's grip now.

What Is the "World System"?

When Scripture speaks of *the world*, it's not referencing geography or humanity in general, it's describing a system. A spiritual and cultural framework that resists the reign of Christ and seduces the hearts of people. It's the unseen network of ideas, values, priorities, and influences that form a counterfeit kingdom.

The world system is both visible and invisible. It operates through culture, media, education, government, art, religion, and more. It's not random; it's orchestrated.

"The whole world lies under the sway of the evil one." —1 John 5:19

That's why Satan had the audacity to offer Jesus all the kingdoms of the world and their glory if He would only bow down (Matthew 4:8–9). It wasn't a bluff; Satan had them to offer. These earthly kingdoms and systems are under his influence, not because he owns the earth, but because humanity gave away authority through sin, and he's been shaping the world's agenda and system ever since.

The systems and kingdoms of this world are:

Opposed to God's will

Rooted in pride and self-exaltation

Driven by power, greed, control, and deception

Designed to distract, deceive, and dominate

Every domain touched by this system from entertainment to education, religion to relationships is subtly (or blatantly) pulling us away from the Kingdom of God. It glorifies:

Independence over surrender

Appearance over authenticity

Comfort over calling

The temporary over the eternal

The world system is Babylon in disguise. It builds towers of pride while rejecting the presence of God.

In Scripture, *Babylon* is more than just an ancient city, it's a symbol of the world's systems operating apart from God. It represents culture, power structures, and values that are under the sway of the evil one (1 John 5:19). Babylon is the counterfeit kingdom operating seductively, self-servingly, and spiritually toxic while it builds on pride, greed, control, and human strength. In contrast, the Kingdom of God calls us to humble surrender and allegiance to Jesus. Babylon calls us to self-exaltation and allegiance to anything but Christ. To live as citizens of God's Kingdom means we must come out of Babylon not just physically, but spiritually and ideologically as well. We can't live by the world's systems and walk in Kingdom authority.

This is why Jesus said, *"My Kingdom is not of this world"* (John 18:36). His Kingdom doesn't play by the world's rules or operate in its power structures. It's upside-down. It's inside-out. It's *other*.

The world and everything it comprises is like a river with a relentless current. It's always moving, always pushing, always pulling in one direction: away from God's Kingdom. You don't have to try to drift; the current does the work for you. It shapes your thoughts, values, priorities, and affections without asking permission. That's the nature of the world system: subtle, persuasive, pervasive, and spiritually dangerous. And if we're not resisting the pull, we're probably already drifting.

Following Jesus is more than just resisting the current. His Kingdom isn't a better path in the river; it's a Rock that stands above it. Christ is the immovable foundation; the solid ground we build our lives upon. While the world rushes by with its pressures, trends, and temptations, the Rock remains. The current may swirl, pull, and rage around us, but those who stand on the Rock are not swept away. We don't just survive the current, we rise above it. The Kingdom of God is not subject to the flow of culture; it is anchored in the unchanging reign of Christ. You won't blend in. You'll stand out and that's exactly the point. The Kingdom life isn't about escaping the world but living in it as light, anchored in a different reality, under a different rule.

Religion: A System of This World

We talked in Chapter 2 about religion vs relationship. Religion often presents itself as good, but it is still a man-made system that quite often, operates apart from God, driven by pride, fear, and control. Let's be very clear: religion is a system of this world.

It might wear spiritual clothing, it might speak the name of God, but when it operates apart from the life of Christ and the Spirit of God, religion becomes nothing more than Babylon repackaged. A false kingdom dressed up in holy language.

Religion is, at its core, a world system cloaked in spiritual talk and imagery. It mimics the Kingdom but is rooted in the flesh. It preaches morality but promotes self-righteousness. It demands conformity but resists true transformation.

This isn't a new problem. It's as old as Babel itself, where humanity first tried to reach heaven on its own terms (Genesis 11:4). It showed up again in Jesus' day through the Pharisees—men who had the scriptures but missed the Messiah standing in front of them. And it continues today in churches that are more committed to tradition, control, or image than to Christ.

Make no mistake: this is not the work of God. It's the enemy's most subtle and sinister strategy. If he can't keep you from seeking God, he'll try to get you to settle for a version of God wrapped in religion but void of life. Satan doesn't just oppose the Kingdom; he actively counterfeits it.

The result?
A long, tragic history of damage done in God's name:
Wars justified by theology
Abuse hidden behind pulpits
Oppression and fear cloaked as obedience
Systems built to control rather than shepherd

This is not the way of Jesus.

Revelation pulls back the curtain and shows us what this religious system truly is: Babylon the Great, the harlot that deceives the nations (Revelation 17–18). It may look impressive on the outside, but its foundation is pride, and its destiny is judgment.

That's why heaven issues a clear call:

"Come out of her, My people, so that you will not share in her sins..." — Revelation 18:4

The Church was never meant to be a religious institution. The **ekklesia** is a *called-out people*, living under a different King, shaped by a different Spirit, and aligned with a different culture—the culture of Heaven.

Religion builds towers
The Kingdom builds people
Religion protects power
The Kingdom empowers love
Religion enslaves
The Kingdom sets free

So, if you've been burned by religion, know this: Jesus didn't come to start a religion. He came to end the tyranny of all religious systems and open the way to real life, life in Him. What He builds is not another version of the world's system. It's something entirely new: a Kingdom not of this world, where love reigns, truth sets free, and grace transforms.

Come out of the system. Come into the Kingdom.

Jesus Lived Set Apart

Though Jesus walked among the people, shared their meals, entered their villages, and touched their wounds; He was never defined by their systems. He didn't climb the ladders of power. He didn't play political games. He wasn't shaped by culture or swayed by crowds.

Jesus never sought influence the way the world chases it through platform, popularity, or performance. In fact, He often withdrew when people tried to make Him king on their terms (John 6:15). His authority wasn't taken; it was given by the Father. His mission wasn't to reform the old order but to introduce an entirely new Kingdom.

When Satan tempted Him by offering "all the kingdoms of the world and their glory" (Luke 4:5–7), Jesus didn't just resist. He rejected the entire premise. Why? Because He didn't come to inherit the corrupted kingdoms of man. He came to establish the unshakable Kingdom of God.

Jesus was the freest man who ever lived because He belonged entirely to another realm.

"They are not of the world, just as I am not of the world." — John 17:16

He was in the world, but not of it. And now, He calls us to the same life— not a life of escape or fear, but of holy distinction. Our values, our choices, our loves, our allegiances—are to be shaped by His Kingdom, not this world's system.

To follow Jesus means:
We say no to the shortcut of doing it my way and yes to surrender.
We resist the pull of culture and respond to the call of Christ.
We walk in boldness, not to fit in, but to stand out in love, truth, and grace.

Jesus didn't die so you could blend in. He died so you could be reborn into a new way of being, a new Kingdom, a new heart, and a new allegiance.

A Better Kingdom, A Better King

It's impossible not to be influenced by the world's system. Its patterns are everywhere woven into our news feeds, entertainment, education, economy, and even religion. Whether we realize it or not, the world is constantly discipling us by shaping our values, our goals, our identities. You can't live in Babylon and not inhale its air. That's why trying to resist the world with your own strength is futile. The only way to break free is to renounce your connection and give your allegiance to a different Kingdom with a better King.

My friend, *that* Kingdom is what God has been establishing from the beginning. It's His Kingdom, and Christ is its only King. This Kingdom doesn't operate by the world's system. It isn't influenced by its corruption or in league with its ruler. Jesus declared, *"The prince of this world is coming. He has no hold on Me"* (John 14:30). In Him there is no compromise, no mixture, no alliance with the powers of darkness.

In every way, the Kingdom of God is better. Just as the book of Hebrews proclaims: a *better covenant*, a *better sacrifice*, a *better priest*, a *better promise*, and yes, a *better King*. His name is Jesus.

Unlike the rulers of this world, He lays down His life for His people. He doesn't manipulate. He transforms. He doesn't demand allegiance out of fear but invites loyalty through love. He is not a tyrant to be appeased but a King to be adored.

"Therefore, since we are receiving a Kingdom that cannot be shaken, let us be thankful, and so worship God acceptably with reverence and awe." — Hebrews 12:28

"The goal of the Gospel isn't just to get you to Heaven. It's to get Heaven back into you, so you stop living like this world is your home." – Dan Mohler

My Own Awakening

For much of my time in ministry, I assumed we could "redeem" the world's systems by Christianizing them. If we just had enough dynamic preaching, good services, and the right systems; surely that would be enough, so I prayed longer, tried harder, and planned deeper. But eventually, I started to feel exasperated. The pace, pressure, and priorities I had accepted as ministry were making me tired, distracted, empty, and shallow. I was chasing fruit but not abiding in the Vine (John 15:5). I was measuring success like the world did through numbers, visibility, and relevance.

The Spirit began to convict me gently but clearly: *You're using the world's tools to build My Kingdom. That's not freedom. That's mixture.*

I realized I didn't just need to resist sin. I needed to renounce the *systems*.

Signs You're Still Tied to the World

You feel anxious when you're not in control

When the world is your anchor, uncertainty breeds fear. You constantly feel the need to manage, manipulate, or micromanage every outcome because if you're not in control, everything feels like it could fall apart. In the Kingdom, peace isn't found in control, but in trust. The more you know the King, the less you panic when things go sideways.

You constantly compare your life to others

Comparison is the world's measuring stick. Social media makes it worse. Someone's highlight reel often becomes a source of insecurity and contrast. In the Kingdom, your identity isn't shaped by how you stack up; it's secured in who Christ says you are. When you know your place in the Kingdom, envy has no room to grow.

You measure your value by what you produce or how you're perceived

The world says your worth is in your hustle, but Kingdom citizens don't perform for value, they live from it. You are not the sum of your successes, your productivity, or your likes. You're a beloved son or daughter of the King. Your value was settled at the cross, not on a scoreboard.

You chase things Jesus never told you to seek

Chasing fame, status, comfort, and security these are the things world glorifies, but Jesus said to *"seek first the Kingdom."* If your pursuit is draining your soul or distracting your purpose, it's time to ask: Did Jesus call me to this, or did the world sell it to me? Not every good-looking opportunity is a God-ordained one and not all good things are God things.

You talk more about your goals than His glory

There's nothing wrong with dreams but when they become the center of your conversations, your prayers, or your decisions, it's worth asking: *Whose Kingdom am I building?* In the world, ambition is a badge of honor. In the Kingdom, surrender is. Goals are only great if they kneel to His glory.

Freedom doesn't come from trying harder. It comes from living under a different government, the rule and reign of King Jesus. His Kingdom doesn't enslave you to anxiety, comparison, or performance. It frees you to live secure, surrendered, and full of purpose. When Jesus is King, freedom isn't a concept. It's your new reality.

You confuse political allegiance with Kingdom loyalty

Politics is one of the most seductive substitutes for Kingdom identity. It promises power, control, and change, but it often ends up demanding your allegiance in ways only Jesus deserves. When your mood, hope, or sense of peace rises and falls with election results or government decisions, it is a sign the world's system still has too much of your heart. Earthly kingdoms come and go. They legislate, they argue, and they shift with public opinion. But the Kingdom of God does not need a party platform to advance. It grows in hearts, not in halls of power. Be engaged but not entangled. Vote with wisdom, but do not anchor your faith to outcomes. Jesus is not running for office, and His throne is not up for election. Your hope must be built on His unshakable rule, not the success or failure of human governments.

You feed on entertainment but starve your spirit

Entertainment is one of the most subtle ways the world dulls our hunger for God. What we consume shapes what we crave. If hours disappear scrolling, streaming, and binge-watching while prayer, Scripture, and fellowship feel like chores, something deeper is happening. Entertainment is not evil, but it becomes dangerous when it numbs our sensitivity to the Spirit or distracts us from our purpose. The world sells constant stimulation to keep you from stillness, because stillness is where you hear God's voice. It fills your life with noise, so you never have to face the deeper hunger inside you. In the Kingdom, joy and rest are not found in constant distraction but in communion with the King. What you feed will grow. Starve the noise, and you will begin to crave His presence again.

You chase secret knowledge more than simple obedience

Conspiracy culture promises deeper insight, hidden truth, and insider knowledge. It flatters the ego by making you feel like you know what is really going on. But chasing endless theories can lead to suspicion, fear, and pride, which are the very opposite of the fruit of the Spirit. It shifts your focus from God's revealed truth to humanity's speculations. The irony is that Jesus never called us to unravel every mystery of the world. He called us to trust Him, obey Him, and proclaim His Kingdom. If conspiracy videos consume your nights more than Scripture shapes your days, or if you are more passionate about exposing darkness than embodying light, it may be time to repent of misplaced curiosity. The deepest truth you will ever know is not hidden in a thread or a headline. It is found in the person of Christ, who is Himself the Truth.

What Does Kingdom Freedom Look Like?

Identity from Christ, Not Culture

You are not what you do.
You are not what you've done.
You are not what others say about you.

The world will try to convince you otherwise. Culture screams, "Define yourself. Brand yourself. Prove yourself." It tells you that your worth is tied to your résumé, your appearance, your likes, your influence, your bank account, or your credit score. And if people approve and applaud, we mask ourselves in a sense of accomplished identity.

But in the Kingdom, identity isn't achieved. It's received.

In Christ, your identity is not based on performance, it's based on position. You are not climbing a ladder to earn significance; you're standing on the unshakable foundation of being chosen, adopted, redeemed, and sealed. (Ephesians 1:3–14)

The gospel doesn't just rescue you from sin, it redefines who you are. You're not an orphan looking for approval. You're a son or daughter of the King. You don't have to hustle for validation; you already have His affection. You don't need to build your identity on shifting sand, it's been secured by the finished work of Jesus.

This isn't self-esteem, it's Christ-esteem. Confidence that flows from who He is and who you are in Him.

This Kingdom identity frees you from the exhausting game of comparison. You no longer need to compare your life to someone else's highlight reel or prove that you're enough. You're free to live authentically, boldly, and purposefully not to gain worth, because you already have it.

When you know who you are in Christ, the voices of culture lose their power. You no longer live to be seen. You live from being known, known by the One who made you, saved you, and calls you His own.

Peace that Defies Circumstances

The world says peace is the absence of problems. It promises peace through perfect conditions, a healthy bank account, a drama-free life, stable emotions, and everything going your way. But that kind of peace is fragile, it cracks under pressure. One unexpected bill, one bad report, one broken relationship and it's gone.

Jesus offers something entirely different.

He says peace isn't found in the absence of trouble but in *His presence within it*. "My peace I give to you, not as the world gives..." (John 14:27). This isn't a pep talk or a positive mindset. It's a supernatural calm rooted in the unshakable reality of who Jesus is. Kingdom peace doesn't deny problems; it declares that Jesus is greater than them.

This kind of peace is anchored. It's not tied to your mood or your circumstances; it's tethered to a Person. It's the confidence that even in the storm, Jesus is in the boat. Even when the diagnosis comes, He's still the Healer. Even when you don't understand, He is still faithful. Kingdom peace isn't the absence of chaos, but it is the presence of Christ in the middle of it, and He is King over all!

When you live under His rule, your heart learns to be still, not because everything is calm on the outside, but because the King reigns on the inside. The same Jesus who calmed the wind and waves now calms the anxious storm within you. This peace can't be manufactured or faked. It's cultivated by abiding in Him, trusting Him, and refusing to let fear become your guide.

This is the kind of peace the world can't produce; it's the kind of peace that makes the world take notice.

Simplicity Over Striving

The world says hustle harder, do more, climb faster. It measures worth in busyness, applauds exhaustion, and equates constant activity with success. The pace is relentless with a grind that demands more and more while delivering less and less peace. It's a performance treadmill that never stops and never satisfies.

The Kingdom whispers a different invitation: *"Come to Me and rest."* (Matthew 11:28–30)

In the Kingdom, your value isn't found in what you can accomplish but in whom you belong to. You don't earn your way into favor; you live from it.

Jesus never called us to a life of burnout; He called us to abide. Striving leads to spiritual depletion, abiding leads to fruit that remains.

Kingdom freedom calls you off the hamster wheel of performance and into the grace of simplicity. A life that is focused on the essential: loving God and loving others. It's not laziness; it's alignment. When you walk with Jesus, simplicity isn't about having less, it's about needing less: less approval, less achievement, and less noise. Why? Because *He is enough.*

Simplicity in the Kingdom means trusting that Jesus is better at carrying the weight than you are. It's choosing to rest, not because everything is done, but because everything that *needs* to be done has already been finished at the cross. Rest isn't weakness, it's worship! It's a declaration that God is in control, and you are not a slave to what the systems of this world deem as success.

This is the kind of life that bears fruit not through frantic effort, but through rooted trust.

Generosity Over Greed

The world says, "Protect what's yours. Look out for number one." We're taught from an early age to accumulate, to compete, and to clutch tightly to what we have, just in case. The Kingdom of God, however, operates on an entirely different economy, one that's not built on scarcity but on abundance. In the Kingdom, generosity isn't optional. It's a natural response to the overwhelming grace we've received.

Jesus doesn't guilt you into giving; He empowers you with the joy of it. He doesn't say, "Give or else," but rather, "Look how much you've already been given." He turns giving from an obligation into an opportunity, a joy-filled expression of trust in the Father's provision.

"Freely you have received, freely give" (Matthew 10:8). This isn't just a principle; it's a Kingdom posture.

It's not just about money. It's about a lifestyle. A way of living with open hands and an open heart. Kingdom generosity flows into how you spend your time, how you use your talents, how you open your home, how you listen, how you serve, and how you love, even when it costs you something.

When you give generously, you declare with your life that *God is enough.* You expose greed for what it is. A lie that says you are your own provider. Generosity silences the fear that says, there won't be enough and replaces it with the truth: My Father owns it all, and He's not stingy.

In a world consumed by getting, Kingdom citizens are marked by giving; a radical, joyful, countercultural giving not to earn approval, but to display the nature of our generous King. When we live this way, generosity becomes worship, and giving becomes a witness to the One who gave it all.

Holiness as Wholeness

Holiness isn't about being weird, cold, or detached. It's not walking around with a spiritual superiority complex or avoiding the world in fear of "contamination." That's not holiness, that's religion wrapped in insecurity. True holiness isn't stiff or somber; it's vibrant, life-giving, and joyful. It's not about isolating yourself from the world; it's about being distinct within it.

In the Kingdom, holiness isn't a burden. It's a blessing! It's not a rigid list of dos and don'ts, but a way of being that reflects the nature of the King Himself. Holiness is wholeness. It's living in sync with the way you were designed. It's what happens when your heart, mind, and body align under the loving rule of Christ. You're not fractured by sin or driven by shame, instead you're rooted in purpose, peace, and purity.

To be holy means to be set apart, not just *from* something, but *for* something. Set apart for intimacy with God, set apart for love, and set apart for living a way that actually looks like Jesus. Holiness is not about being *better than*, it's about being *fully His.*

When you walk closely with the Holy One, you start to reflect Him. His values shape your choices. His Spirit reshapes your desires. Little by little, His beauty is formed in you. 1 Peter 1:15–16 reminds us, "Just as He who called you is holy, so be holy in all you do." Not out of fear, but out of freedom, because holiness isn't about perfection, it's about devotion.

Story: When the World's Success Leaves You Empty

I once knew a man who checked all the boxes of worldly success. He built a thriving business, was respected in his industry, admired in his church, and known for his charisma and drive. He gave faithfully, attended regularly, and even spoke at church events—usually about leadership, excellence, and maximizing your potential for God.

On the surface, everything looked impressive: big numbers, strong influence, and growing opportunity. But beneath the applause, something was unraveling.

In his relentless pursuit of success, something sacred was slipping away. His marriage began to fracture—slowly at first, then painfully. His wife felt emotionally abandoned. His children drifted away, resentful of a father whose time and attention always seemed just out of reach. Eventually, his marriage collapsed. His kids stopped calling—except when money was involved.

He didn't lose everything overnight; the world's system is more subtle than that. It applauds your effort while it drains your soul. It promises meaning but leaves you empty. And then it offers one more fix, one more project, one more platform, one more promotion—anything to keep you from facing what's really broken.

Even now, in the silence left behind by all he lost, the world hasn't stopped whispering. It still lures him with new promises: the next big deal, the next reinvention, the next opportunity to prove he's still "got it." It tells him he can still fix it all if he just runs a little harder, climbs a little higher. And he still chases after it.

The truth is, he doesn't need a platform or program, he needs peace. He doesn't need a second wind; he needs a new kingdom.

I pray for him often. That the noise will quiet, that the veil will lift. That he'll see the system for what it really is just Babylon in a business suit. I pray that he'll realize Jesus isn't looking for his productivity, but offering him presence, redemption, and a reset.

Because even now, after all the loss and all the regret his story isn't over. Jesus is still standing on the shore. Still calling his name. Still ready with grace. The world celebrates performance and punishes failure, but the Kingdom welcomes the broken.

I truly believe that his story and countless others like it can still be rewritten by the author and finisher of our faith!

Jesus Didn't Fit In

Jesus didn't come to be accepted by the world. He came to overturn it. He wasn't impressive by the world's standards: He had no title, no wealth, no political backing. *"He had no beauty or majesty to attract us to Him"* (Isaiah 53:2). He didn't network for influence, He called fishermen. He didn't climb ladders, He washed feet. He didn't defend His image, but instead He bore our shame.

He was misunderstood by the religious, rejected by the powerful, and abandoned by the crowd. Yet He stayed faithful to His mission, because His allegiance was never to popularity or applause. It was to the Father.

"If the world hates you, remember it hated Me first... You do not belong to the world. That is why the world hates you."
—*John 15:18–19*

To live in the Kingdom of God is to live counter to culture just like Jesus did. It means choosing humility over hype, service over status, truth over trend, and obedience over opinion. The Kingdom doesn't run on visibility, algorithms, or applause. It runs on love, sacrifice, and surrender.

The more we walk in step with Jesus, the more out of step we'll be with the world. That's not a failure, it's freedom.

True freedom means we're no longer trying to gain acceptance from a system that runs on pride, performance, and power. We're no longer trying to belong where we were never meant to fit. We've been rescued from one kingdom and transferred into another (Colossians 1:13).

The Kingdom of God doesn't seek to fit in because it exists to stand out.

Entering the Kingdom

You don't drift into the Kingdom of God; you enter it by surrender. The Gospel of the Kingdom is a summons not a suggestion. It calls you to repent, believe, and bow. Jesus didn't say, "Accept Me into your heart"—He said, *"Follow Me."* Entering the Kingdom means renouncing all rival claims to your allegiance. Things like self, religion, culture, and comfort must all submit to the rule of Christ.

As Frank Viola puts it:
"The Gospel of the Kingdom is not an invitation to pray a prayer and then wait for heaven. It's a call to revolt against the powers that be—the world, the flesh, and the devil—and to give your full allegiance to King Jesus now."

To step into the Kingdom is to defect from the world system. It's not an upgrade to your life; it's the end of your old one.

We'll explore this radical entrance more fully in the next chapter, where we confront what it truly means to live by radical grace and real repentance.

Living This Out

1. Ask What You're Feeding On

→ *What shapes your thinking more, social media or Scripture? What is making the news or the Good News? The patterns you feed are the ones you follow.*

2. Practice Sabbath as Resistance

→ *Rest isn't laziness. It's a declaration: I am not owned by this system. (Exodus 20:8–11) Step away from the grind, do something purposeful with your family and friends. Spend a day enjoying the beauty of God's creation.*

3. Choose Kingdom Over Culture

→ *Let your decisions be led by truth, not trends. Filter your decisions through "What does God's Word say?" not "What is everyone else doing?"*
Holiness, not hype. Guard your inputs—what you watch, listen to, and laugh at—asking if it reflects Kingdom character.
Obedience, not outcomes. Practice generosity (time, finances, encouragement) without expecting recognition

Reflection Questions

1. Where has the world's system shaped your thinking more than the Word?

2. What values are you living by that don't reflect the Kingdom?

3. Are you willing to be "set apart" even when it costs you?

A Prayer for Freedom

Jesus,

I want to live in Your Kingdom not just visit it. I renounce the lies of the world that have shaped my thinking, my habits, and my desires. I receive Your truth, Your way, and Your reign over every part of my life. Teach me how to live free anchored in You, not influenced by this world. I belong to a better Kingdom.

Amen.

---

*The world's system attempts to shape us
through fear and performance.
The Kingdom calls us into something radically different:
grace that transforms and repentance that resurrects.
Let's explore how these two Kingdom gifts change everything*

Chapter 5: Radical Grace and Repentance

**Jesus didn't come to improve your life—
He came to resurrect it.**

"Repent, because the kingdom of heaven has come near."
— *Matthew 4:17*
"God's kindness is intended to lead you to repentance." — *Romans 2:4*
"He who is forgiven much, loves much." — *Luke 7:47*
"For you are saved by grace through faith, and this is not from yourselves; it is God's gift."— *Ephesians 2:8*

Let's be honest, two of the most misunderstood and misused words in the Church today are *grace* and *repent*. Depending on your background and church experience, just hearing those words might stir up some mixed emotions. For some, *grace* has been presented as a license to live however you want, a kind of holy loophole. For others, *repentance* has been tied to shame, fear, or religious performance. These words have been shouted from pulpits, whispered in confessionals, and even weaponized in ways that certainly misrepresent Christ and His word.

But here's the truth: both grace and repentance are powerful Kingdom realities, not religious burdens. When rightly understood, they don't lead us to guilt or apathy; they lead us into freedom and transformation.

Real, Radical Grace

Grace is one of the most misunderstood realities in the Church. We often describe it as "unmerited favor", and it is! Grace is the love, kindness, and acceptance of God freely given to us, not based on our performance, but on Christ's perfection. It's what welcomes the prodigal home, what forgives the deepest sin, and what declares the guilty righteous in the eyes of a holy God.

But that's only half the picture.

Grace isn't just pardon, it's power. It doesn't just free us from sin's penalty; it empowers us to overcome sin's pull. Grace is not permission to remain unchanged. It is the fuel to become who we were always meant to be.

We often lean into the *forgiving* side of grace (and rightly so) but forget that the *transforming* side is just as unearned. We don't overcome sin by trying harder. We don't grow in holiness through sheer willpower. It is *still grace,* God's very life, flowing in us and through us, that enables victory.

"Grace is not the license to sin; it's the liberty to live free." – Dan Mohler

Paul says it plainly in 1 Corinthians 15:10: "But by the grace of God I am what I am, and His grace to me was not without effect."

In other words, grace changes things. It doesn't leave you where it finds you.

God's grace not only meets us in our weakness, but it also moves us forward in strength. Not our own strength, but His. That's what makes grace so radical. It saves, it sustains, and it sanctifies. It's all grace from beginning to end.

Grace That Offends Religion

Grace is radical because it's not fair. It's offensive to religious minds because it dares to forgive fully, love unconditionally, and restore freely.

Grace is scandalous. Not because it's weak, but because it's wildly undeserved. It mocks the religiously aligned because it can't be earned, managed, or measured. Grace forgives what religion wants to punish. It restores what legalism says should remain broken. It embraces the prodigal while the elder brother still stands outside fuming.

Religious systems are built by merit on doing more, trying harder, and proving worth. They want repentance to look like punishment, transformation to come through shame, and favor to be bought with behavior. Kingdom grace flips the script. It doesn't hand out spiritual gold stars for good performance. It lays a feast for the failures, it throws its arms around the undeserving and it runs toward the repentant, not away.

Religion says, "Work harder."
Grace says, "It is finished."

Religion demands proof of receipt.
Grace gives promise of His presence.

Religion waits for you to clean up.
Grace meets you in the mud and walks you home.

Jesus didn't come offering rules. He came offering relationship built on mercy and truth; the kind of relationship that doesn't keep score, doesn't shame, and doesn't give up.

Grace is so hard for religion to accept, because control is lost, power structures crumble, and no one gets to boast. But this is exactly what makes grace so beautiful, it levels the ground, lifts the humble, and reveals a Kingdom built not on ladders, but on love.

Real, Radical Repentance

We often think of repentance as sorrow, feeling bad for what we've done, but the Greek word used in Scripture is **metanoia**, meaning a complete change of mind and direction. It's not about emotional regret. It's about realigning with God's original purpose for us. It's awakening to the truth that I've been living under the wrong rule, chasing the wrong goals, and trusting the wrong source.

Real repentance doesn't say, *"I'm a mess, so I better try harder."*
It says, *"I've seen the truth, and I surrender to it."*

We weren't created to live from self.
We were made to live from the indwelling life of Christ.

When we repent, we are trading the lie of independence for the life of connection with Christ.

Repentance is not about wallowing in failure. It's waking up to the fact that you were made for more. That Christ in you, is the hope of glory!

And let's be clear: Repentance is not a cycle of constant confession and begging for forgiveness. Sin is a solved problem because of the cross. Jesus' blood wasn't partial, it was perfect.

The Bible never tells us to ask repeatedly for what has already been freely given. Instead, it tells us to confess, to agree with God about what is true.

"If we confess our sins, He is faithful and just to forgive us our sins and to cleanse us from all unrighteousness." (1 John 1:9)

Confession is not about *getting* God to forgive.
It's about *receiving* what He already gave.

If we find ourselves constantly confessing the same sin without change, we're not living in repentance; we're living in religion. Because true repentance doesn't just stop behavior, it starts transformation.

Repentance leads to resurrection—a new mind, a new heart, and a new life.

Repentance is not a revolving door of guilt. It's a gateway to glory.

Repentance Isn't Groveling

In the Kingdom, repentance is not shame driven. It's identity shifting.

Repentance isn't about self-loathing, it's not groveling at God's feet, hoping for mercy, nor is it replaying our failures on repeat.

Repentance is awakening. It's realigning. It's returning.

True repentance is the joyful surrender of self-rule in light of the goodness of Christ's rule.

It's not about getting stuck in guilt; it is about being drawn into grace.
It's not the product of fear but the fruit of seeing Jesus rightly.
As Paul wrote, it's *"God's kindness that leads us to repentance"* (Romans 2:4).

Repentance isn't just saying I'm sorry.
It's saying, yes, Jesus. You can have it all.

This is why real repentance leads to real resurrection power.
When we turn from ourselves and turn fully to Christ, we don't just get forgiven, we get filled.

Filled with His Spirit
Filled with His nature
Filled with His Kingdom

A Story of Return: A Robe, A Ring, and a Ribeye Steak

Nowhere is the fusion of grace and repentance more vivid than in Jesus' parable of the prodigal son in Luke 15.

The younger son, often called the prodigal, didn't just make a mistake. He committed a cultural and relational betrayal. In asking for his inheritance early, he was essentially saying to his father, *"I'd rather you be dead so I can have your stuff."* Then he took that inheritance and wasted it on reckless, self-centered living. What began in thrill ended in famine. What looked like freedom turned to slavery. He found himself broke, starving, and feeding pigs—a job so degrading it was considered unclean for any Jew.

But notice what brings him back.

It wasn't guilt.
It wasn't condemnation.
It was hope. A memory of the goodness of his father.
He rehearsed a humble speech: *"I am no longer worthy to be called your son. Make me like one of your hired servants..."* (Luke 15:19)

But he never got to finish the speech. While he was still a long way off, the father saw him. Because the father had never stopped watching the horizon. Instead of crossing his arms in judgment, he ran—something undignified for a man of his age and stature. The son was dirty, smelly, and broken; and yet He ran, embraced, and kissed him.

Then the gifts came.

A Robe – the best one in the house. This wasn't a bathrobe to cover dirt; it was a symbol of honor. The son came in shame, but the robe declared him covered, welcomed, and wanted.

A Ring – not a trinket, but a signet ring, a symbol of authority and belonging. It meant the son could now sign in the father's name again. From rebellion to reinstatement, without a probationary period. The father was declaring, *"You are not a servant. You are my child."*

And a Ribeye Steak – okay, it was a fattened calf, but let's be honest: in our terms, it's the good stuff. This wasn't fast food. This was reserved for the most special of occasions. A celebration of relationship restored. The father didn't demand an apology or assign chores. He threw a party.

"Bring the best... Let's eat and celebrate. For this son of mine was dead and is alive again; he was lost and is found." (Luke 15:23–24)

Jesus didn't tell this story to showcase a sinner's failure.
He told it to reveal the Father's heart and the true nature of the Kingdom.

But the story doesn't end there. The older brother, dutiful, hardworking, but offended, refused to join the celebration.

He represents religion: Keeping score. Demanding fairness. Missing joy because of judgment.

He had proximity to the father but no intimacy with him.
He had access to the house but didn't carry the heart of his Father. He knew the rules of belonging but not the joy of relationship

Grace offends the religious mindset because it can't be earned or controlled. It celebrates return instead of punishing rebellion. It gives honor back to failures. It throws feasts instead of handing out fines.

And that's the scandal of Kingdom grace.

The only person who remained outside the celebration was the one who believed he had done everything right.

Religion demands better behavior.
The Kingdom births a new heart.

Repentance and Grace: The Pathway to Resurrection Life

Repentance and grace are not at odds. They are deeply intertwined. You cannot truly experience one without the other. Real repentance opens the door, and radical grace floods in and transforms everything.

Remember that the Greek word used in the Bible for repentance, *metanoia*, means "a change of mind"—but not just a shift in thought. It's a reorientation of the heart, a complete turning from the patterns of this world toward the Person of Christ. It's not driven by guilt or shame, but by the revelation that we were made for something more and for Someone greater.

Repentance says:

I've been living under the wrong rule, chasing the wrong goals.

I wasn't created to live for self, I was made to be filled with Christ.

I return to Christ not because I'm afraid, but because I see clearly now.

This is the moment grace rushes in.

Grace is unearned in offering forgiveness and in empowerment.

- It pardons the sinner
- It raises the dead
- It empowers the weak
- It produces Kingdom life

True grace isn't lowering the bar; true grace raises dead hearts to life.

Titus 2:11–12 says that the grace of God teaches us to say 'No' to ungodliness. In other words: Grace is not permission to sin. It's power to be free.

Repentance is the yes that makes space, and Grace is the power that fills it. Jesus didn't come just to forgive you; He came to fill you with His life. The cross was the cost and resurrection is the result, and repentance is the doorway that brings you from death to life. You don't just get a second chance. You get a new heart, a new spirit, a new Kingdom, and a new identity.

"Therefore, if anyone is in Christ, he is a new creation; the old has passed away, and see, the new has come!" — 2 Corinthians 5:17

This is the power of repentance and grace together:

Repentance brings surrender

Grace brings strength

Repentance turns from self

Grace empowers life in Christ

Repentance brings you home

Grace clothes you in righteousness and invites you to stay.

You're not just forgiven. You're free. You're not just restored. You're resurrected. You're not just a sinner saved by grace. You are a citizen of the Kingdom, filled with resurrection power and sealed with the Spirit of the Living God.

Repentance is not about constantly looking backward at what you did wrong. It's about continually turning your eyes to the One who makes all things new.

Repentance isn't groveling. It's surrendering.

Grace isn't soft, it's supernatural. When they meet, you don't just change.

You come alive.

There's More to the Story

I was once asked to speak at a men's recovery home. It was a room full of men who had tasted rock bottom. Many battling addictions, regret, and the weight of lost years. As I shared about the hope found in Christ, one man stood up to give his testimony.

He said he used to run a successful painting business. Then came the contract with a massive deal that instantly made him a millionaire. It should have been the breakthrough that changed everything, but instead, it was the beginning of his unraveling. Alcohol and drug use crept in. He lost his focus, then his business. Eventually, he lost all his wealth, his family, his job, and his home.

Now he was living in that recovery house on limited finances. And yet, with tears in his eyes, he said, "But I found Christ and He forgave me."

That was where he ended the story.

As I looked around that room, something stirred in me. I didn't doubt the sincerity of his faith, or the beauty of his forgiveness. But I couldn't help but say, *"Friend, that's not the end of the story, it's only the beginning."*

Grace is more than a pardon from the past. It's power for the future.

The Gospel isn't just about not going to hell; it's about entering a Kingdom. It's not just getting clean; it's being made new. Repentance leads us out of shame, but grace leads us into the glory of Christ's kingdom and the strength of His reign.

You weren't saved to stay stuck.

You were redeemed for a purpose, called into a Kingdom, and invited into sonship.

The past isn't your story. Christ and His Kingdom are your story, where grace and repentance lead to the riches of His glory in Christ Jesus (Philippians 4:19).

God doesn't just wipe the board clean. He writes a whole new future. One where resurrection life flows through your veins. One where your identity isn't the man who lost it all, but the son who's been given it all in Christ.

And that's a story worth living.

Signs You've Met Grace but Missed the Kingdom

Grace is often preached as the open door, but the Kingdom is what lies beyond it. Too many stop at the threshold, forgiven but not free. Loved, yet still living like spiritual orphans. You may have received grace intellectually but never walked into the full reality of life in the Kingdom.

Here are a few signs:

You still feel unworthy, even after forgiveness.
You believe God forgave you but secretly wonder if He really likes you. You walk with your head down, like a guest in God's house rather than a child in His family.

You try to earn God's approval through performance.
You know grace in theory, but in practice you're still striving and trying to prove you're enough. Your prayers feel like pressure. Your service feels like a debt that you owe. You're saved, but still working like you're on probation.

You confuse conviction with condemnation.
Instead of the Spirit's gentle correction, you hear the voice of shame. You feel accused, not invited. Exposed, but not embraced. You think God's always disappointed with you; forgetting that conviction is rooted in love, not judgment.

You serve more out of fear than love.
Your motivation is avoiding God's wrath, not enjoying His presence. You obey out of obligation rather than intimacy. You say "yes" to God, but deep down, it's not joy, it's duty.

But here's the truth: Grace is not soft or weak.
It's not a cute sympathy card.
It's ferocious love that *rescues*, *transforms*, and *restores*.

It doesn't just pardon you; it prepares a place for you.
It doesn't just invite you in; it calls you beloved.

It doesn't just save you from judgment; it sends you with authority.
It doesn't just open the door; it places the keys in your hands.

If grace gets you out of Egypt, the Kingdom is where you learn to live free in the Promised Land.

The Spirit you received does not make you slaves, so that you live in fear again; rather, the Spirit you received brought about your adoption to sonship.

If grace has reached you yet you still feel bound by striving, hear the Father's call: Come further in. Mercy opens the door and majesty awaits inside

---

Living in Grace, Walking in Repentance

Grace and repentance are not just the entry point into the Kingdom. They are the *ongoing rhythm* of Kingdom life.

They aren't boxes to check off at salvation or emotions we revisit at altar calls. They are a daily way of walking, a lifestyle of surrender and transformation.

Repentance isn't a return to shame. It's a return to the King. It's not driven by our guilt but drawn by His glory.

And grace? Grace doesn't just pardon from sin, it gives power for transformation. It doesn't excuse who you've been, but it empowers who you're becoming.

We're not changed by striving harder.
We're changed by seeing Jesus rightly.

"We all, with unveiled faces, are looking as in a mirror at the glory of the Lord and are being transformed into the same image from glory to glory..." — *2 Corinthians 3:18*

This is the rhythm of real Kingdom life:

Grace welcomes us in. Repentance realigns our hearts. And then His Glory transforms our lives.

The more you behold Him, the more you become like Him.
The more you abide in grace, the more repentance becomes joy and not shame. You stop asking How close can I get to sin? and start asking How close can I stay to Jesus?

A Better Kingdom with a Better King

The world offers two paths, both equally bankrupt:

Shame-based religion, where you endlessly strive but never arrive.
Self-justifying rebellion, where you do what feels good, but end up empty.

But Jesus offers a *third way*. A better Kingdom, ruled by a better King.

In this Kingdom, grace is the foundation and repentance is the doorway.
You don't enter by merit. You enter by mercy.
You don't earn your way in. You *surrender* your way in.

Jesus didn't come to improve your personality or polish your habits.
He came to make you new, to replace your old self with His very life.

He didn't die just to get you into heaven. He died to get heaven into *you*.
To fill your life with resurrection power. To form you not as a rule-keeping servant, but as a beloved son or daughter of the King.

"But to all who did receive him, he gave them the right to be children of God ..." — John 1:12

That's the difference between religion and the Kingdom:

Religion modifies behavior.

The Kingdom grants new identity.

And in the Kingdom, transformation is not about trying harder.
It's about living from the new nature Christ has placed within you.

This is the *Kingdom* Jesus announced:
A better Kingdom
A better covenant
A better hope
And a better King

"But Jesus has now obtained a superior ministry, and to that degree he is the mediator of a better covenant, which has been established on better promise."
— *Hebrews 8:6*

You don't need to chase the world's validation. You don't need to live ashamed or strive for approval. You can trade it all for a Kingdom that cannot be shaken, and a King who cannot fail.

Living This Out

This Kingdom isn't just something we believe in. It's something we live. Grace and repentance become the rhythm of our everyday walk, not just moments at an altar. So how do we live it out?

1. Confess Often
→*Repentance isn't weakness, it's freedom in motion.*
It's not shame-driven groveling, but Spirit-led surrender.
It's admitting, "Your way is better, King Jesus. I trust You more than I trust myself."

Ask daily:
"Where am I still holding the crown? Where am I resisting God's rule in my thoughts, desires, or decisions?"

When we confess, we're not shocking God. We're aligning our hearts with Him.

"If we confess our sins, He is faithful and just to forgive us our sins and to cleanse us from all unrighteousness." — 1 John 1:9

2. Receive Again
→*Grace isn't a one-time gift. It's the fuel of the Kingdom life.*
You don't outgrow it. You grow in it.

Paul told the Galatians; are you now being perfected by the flesh after beginning by the Spirit? (Galatians 3:3).
In other words, don't forget how this started, and don't change how it's sustained. You didn't earn your salvation, and you can't earn your sanctification.

Preach the Gospel to yourself daily. Remind your heart: I am forgiven. I am new. I am empowered. I am beloved.

The grace that saved you is the same grace that sustains you.

3. Restore Others
→*You were never meant to be a container of grace.*
You're meant to be a conduit of it.

If you've been forgiven—forgive.
If you've been loved—love radically.
If you've been restored—be a restorer.

"Brothers and sisters, if someone is overtaken in any wrongdoing, you who are spiritual, restore such a person with a gentle spirit..."
— Galatians 6:1

The Kingdom advances not through domination but through reconciliation. We don't just preach repentance; we create spaces where others can return home. When grace and repentance flow through us, the world doesn't just hear about the Kingdom. They see it.

Reflection Questions

1. Is there an area of your life you're managing instead of surrendering?
2. How do you respond when you fail? With shame or return?
3. How can you extend radical grace to others this week?

A Prayer of Return

Jesus,
I come again not as one who has it all together, but as one in need of Your grace. I turn from my ways and align with Yours. Thank You for the robe, the ring, and the feast. Teach me to walk in grace and live in daily repentance not from guilt, but from love. Be the joy of my heart and the center of my life.
Amen.

Grace doesn't just forgive, it empowers.
Repentance doesn't just turn us around, it sends us out.
The Kingdom life isn't just an inward transformation,
it's outward expression.
Mission isn't a trip you take. It's a life you live.

Chapter 6: Mission as a Lifestyle

Not an Event. A Way of Life.

"As the Father has sent me, I also send you." — *John 20:21*

"make disciples of all nations." — *Matthew 28:18–20*

"You will be my witnesses..." — *Acts 1:8*

"We are ambassadors for Christ." — *2 Corinthians 5:20*

"How will they hear unless someone is sent?" *Romans 10:14–15*

"among whom you shine like stars in the world." — *Philippians 2:15*

Mission isn't primarily about *going*. It's about *being*. It's not a trip you plan; it's a life you live. It's not an outreach; it's shining the light everywhere we go. As Kingdom citizens, we represent Christ's Kingdom wherever we are, because we are *in* His Kingdom, we walk in the light, love, and life of Christ. We don't carry a message as outsiders; we *embody* it as insiders. This means our everyday lives become the mission field: homes, workplaces, grocery stores, trails, and town squares. We are emissaries of the King, not just when we go somewhere special, but *everywhere* we go because of who we are. The mission flows from identity, not itinerary.

More than a mission, it's a continual declaration of the glory of our King and His Kingdom. Our lives are a living testimony to the fact that *His Kingdom is better*. Better than the broken systems of this world. Better than fear, division, and control. We don't just preach the Kingdom, we demonstrate why it's superior. It's faith over fear, love over hate, mercy over judgment and freedom through surrender. Our lives point to the King, and through us, the world gets a glimpse of what life looks like when He reigns.

Not a Trip, But a Trajectory

For many, *mission* is something people go on like a trip, an event, or a scheduled outreach. In the Kingdom, mission isn't an activity, it's an identity.

We are a *sent people*. Every believer is a missionary. Every neighborhood, workplace, coffee shop, or trailhead is sacred ground waiting to be reclaimed by the love of Jesus. Kingdom mission is not something we visit; it's something we live.

Living Sent

Jesus didn't compartmentalize His mission. He was as purposeful at the dinner table as He was in the synagogue. Likewise, mission isn't just what we do, it's how we live.

It's not reserved for the "gifted evangelists" but expressed in the daily faithfulness of Kingdom citizens. When you forgive quickly, that's mission. When you invite the outsider in, that's mission. When we live generously, pray boldly, and love unreasonably, *we are on mission.*

"You weren't just saved from something. You were saved for something. Every day you wake up with breath in your lungs is a day to shine." – Dan Mohler

"The Church's mission isn't church growth. It's Kingdom expression. The measure is not how many we gather, but how much Jesus is seen through us." – Frank Viola

---

A Story from the Pump

It started like any ordinary gas station stop. He was on one side of the pump; I was on the other. We traded a few passing comments about the weather, and maybe a comment or two about the local sports teams. Nothing deep. Nothing "spiritual." Just two strangers filling their tanks.

Then came the shift.

Our conversation wandered to what we did for work. I mentioned I was in the area starting a new church. His posture changed. He paused, looked at me, and said, "My dad used to pastor a church here years ago."

I recognized the name and realized I had met his dad many years before. That simple connection opened a door. I asked about his dad, about his own faith journey, and whether he was connected to a church now.

That's when the divine interrupted the ordinary.

He opened up, I mean *really* opened up. He shared that he hadn't been to church in years—and truthfully, hadn't been following Jesus. Life had happened. Hurts had hardened. He wasn't angry, just distant.

But right there beside that gas pump, the Spirit of God met him. I asked if I could pray with him. He said yes. I prayed for him, for his family, for restoration. He wiped tears from his eyes as the Lord began to stir something in his heart.

I don't know what happened in the days that followed. But I know that moment wasn't an accident.

I didn't do anything extraordinary. I just filled up my truck and stayed present in a conversation. Sometimes, that's all it takes, because that's often where Jesus shows up—right in the middle of the mundane, where hearts are open and Kingdom life flows through simple obedience.

This is what mission as a lifestyle looks like: Not an event, not a program, just a life available to Jesus, every moment, every day.

Kingdom Focus

You are not on mission *for* Jesus. You are on mission *with* Him.
The Great Commission isn't a task list handed down from Heaven. It's an invitation to partnership. Jesus didn't say, "Go and get it done." He said, *"Go... and I will be with you always"* (Matthew 28:20). We're not lone ambassadors working in His absence. We are Spirit-filled sons and daughters walking in His presence. Kingdom mission begins with intimacy, not strategy. When we abide in Him, fruit happens (John 15:5). When we walk with Him, the mission walks through us.

Kingdom mission is relational, not just informational.
We don't win people by convincing them; we win them by loving them. The Gospel is not a sales pitch. It's not about sealing the deal with the right theological formula; it's about revealing Jesus through our lives. People aren't starving for more information; they're starving for transformation, and that transformation is born in the soil of real relationship. Jesus didn't hand out tracts; He handed out time. He embodied truth in the context of trust.

Discipleship happens as we go, not just when we gather.
The early Church didn't grow because they had slick events. It grew because believers shared life. *Day by day... they broke bread in their homes and ate together with glad and sincere hearts* (Acts 2:46). Real discipleship isn't a Wednesday night class. It's a lifestyle. Discipleship happens in car rides, phone calls, coffee shops, and backyard BBQs. It happens when someone sees how you react to stress, how you treat your family, how you live when no one is clapping. The most powerful discipleship moment might be someone watching you live out forgiveness in real time.

Our lives are the message. Our love is the evidence.

Paul wrote, *"You yourselves are our letter, written on our hearts, known and read by everyone"* (2 Corinthians 3:2).

You are the sermon. Your life tells a story about the Kingdom you claim to represent. The evidence of that Kingdom isn't how loudly you preach; it's how deeply you love.

"By this everyone will know that you are my disciples, if you love one another." —John 13:35

Love is not the soft option; it is the strong proof.
It's what makes the Gospel tangible and believable.

Super at the Natural

So many believers miss the mission because they're waiting for something dramatic. We're trained to look for the spectacular, the prophetic word in a service, the vision in a dream, or some undeniable "sign from God." And while God *can* speak through those things, the mission of Jesus rarely starts with flashes of lightning. It starts with *faithfulness in the ordinary.*

Most Kingdom moments aren't staged under spotlights. They're found beside gas pumps, across kitchen tables, and on job sites. We think we need to do something miraculous, but the miracle is often just showing up with a heart available to be used by God. When we carry the Spirit of Christ into normal moments with open hearts and open hands, Heaven invades Earth quietly, but powerfully.

This is exactly how Jesus lived. He didn't stay in synagogues waiting for appointments. He walked, talked, listened, ate, laughed, and wept. He noticed people others overlooked, He asked questions, He shared meals, and through those natural rhythms, the Kingdom was revealed.

The call is not to chase the supernatural, it's to *carry Christ* into the natural. When we do, the supernatural tends to show up.

Colossians 3:17 reminds us: *"And whatever you do, in word or in deed, do everything in the name of the Lord Jesus ..."*

And again in 1 Corinthians 10:31: "So whether you eat or drink or whatever you do, do it all for the glory of God."

That means you can disciple someone while folding laundry, witness to someone while checking out at a store, and change someone's life just by listening well over a cup of coffee.

This world doesn't need more spiritual performers. It needs *present* people; followers of Jesus who walk slowly enough to notice others, love deeply enough to risk rejection, and live humbly enough to know that they're not the miracle. Jesus is!

So, let's stop waiting for the clouds to part. Be super at the natural and trust that the Kingdom comes in jars of clay, not just bolts of lightning.

The Kingdom of God isn't ushered in by outward displays, but by inward devotion. When your heart is surrendered, signs don't need chasing; they naturally follow.

Your World Can Change the World

You don't need a pulpit to preach or a platform to influence. Sometimes, the most powerful Kingdom moments come through the simplest conversations on sidelines, in checkout lines, or at your child's ballgame.

We often underestimate the weight of our words. A question asked with compassion. A prayer offered without fanfare. A word of encouragement spoken at just the right moment—These are not just random interactions; they are holy moments waiting to be recognized.

When you belong to the Kingdom, your heart is open, your ears are listening, and your eyes are alert to what God is doing around you. Your life is the sermon, so every setting becomes sacred.

Here's something I've learned in the last few years: Preaching isn't just proclaiming doctrine from a stage: it's revealing Jesus everyday through love, truth, and being intentionally present.

That's when grocery stores become mission fields, workplaces become altars, and neighborhood walks become Kingdom assignments. Why? Because Christ in you is not limited by location. His Spirit moves wherever you go, and He speaks through your availability.

We don't have to force the Gospel into moments. We simply need to carry it faithfully through them.

Colossians 4:6 reminds us:
"Let your speech always be gracious, seasoned with salt, so that you may know how you should answer each person."

So don't wait for the big stage or the perfect setup. Your world, when surrendered to the Spirit of God, can change someone else's world.

Ministering to Felt Needs

One of the simplest and most powerful ways the Kingdom advances is through compassion.

Jesus didn't just preach the Gospel; He met people where they hurt. He fed the hungry, healed the sick, celebrated life events, touched the leper, and wept with the grieving. His ministry was not confined to a synagogue, but was lived out among people, driven by a heart that felt what others felt.

"When he saw the crowds, he felt compassion for them..." — Matthew 9:36

Ministering to felt needs means responding to the burdens that others are carrying. The ones we can see and those we sense. Sometimes it's a visible need: a financial crisis, an illness, a struggling marriage. Other times it's something you feel: a heaviness in a friend's tone, an emotion in a stranger's eyes, a prompting from the Spirit to ask a simple, "How are you really doing?"

These moments are sacred invitations and when we respond, we become living expressions of Christ's love. If we ignore the pain we see, we deny the presence we carry.

When you step into someone's story with empathy and grace, walls come down, conversations open up, hearts soften, and needs become doorways for prayer, connection, and transformation.

As Paul writes: *"Carry one another's burdens; in this way you will fulfill the law of Christ"* — Galatians 6:2

The Kingdom moves through the hands that reach out, the words that speak life, and the willingness to feel what others feel. Ministry isn't always about just solving problems. It's often about showing up and saying, "You're not alone. Jesus sees you and so do I."

A Glass of Lemonade and the World

A few years ago, at a missions' conference and sending service, I heard a story that has never left me.

A young couple stood on the platform, being commissioned to take the gospel to the nations. The story of how they got there didn't begin with a sermon or a supernatural sign. It started with a stay-at-home mom, two toddlers, and a glass of lemonade.

That mom had wrestled with her place in ministry. Caring for children, managing the home, and rarely leaving the house left her feeling sidelined from God's "real" work. But then she heard a message called, "Your world can change the world."

Something in her heart awakened. Maybe, just maybe, the Kingdom wasn't limited to pulpits and passports. Maybe it could begin right where she stood.

Soon after, her family started receiving frequent package deliveries due to her husband's job. One sweltering summer day, she and her daughters made a pitcher of lemonade and waited for the delivery driver. When he arrived, they offered him a cold drink and a warm smile.

That moment opened the door to many more. Small talk became real conversation. Lemonade led to friendship and friendship led to prayer. Eventually, that driver and his family started attending their life group, found Jesus in a fresh way, and grew in their faith.

A couple of years later, that mom, her husband and her daughters were asked to pray over that delivery driver's family as they were being commissioned into full-time missions.

A few days after that service, the mom saw a delivery truck drive past. On its side, there was a huge image of the globe. As she looked at the image as the van drove by, she felt the whisper of the Holy Spirit: "You thought it was just lemonade. But I used it to touch the world."

This Is the Kingdom

The Kingdom of God does not advance only through sermons or stadiums. It moves through shared interests, open doors, text messages, Tuesday dinners, and gas station conversations.

It's not about titles, talent, or platforms—It's about availability. It's about seeing what's in your hands and trusting that the Spirit of Christ in you is enough to change someone's eternity.

This is how the Kingdom comes.
Not always in power suits or pulpits, but in aprons and errands, in ordinary homes filled with eternal purpose.

This is how the world gets changed.
By disciples who believe that the King truly reigns and who live like He can use anything, even lemonade, to turn the world upside down.

God doesn't need our performance; He wants our presence.

Are you ready to believe that your ordinary moments are holy ground?
Are you ready to live the kind of life that turns water, and sometimes lemonade, into wine?

Because, friend, this is the way of the Kingdom.

As You Go

When Jesus said, *"Go into all the world and make disciples"* (Matthew 28:19), the Greek word for "go" (πορευθέντες – *poreuthentes*) might be better understood to mean "as you go." It isn't simply a command to uproot and move across the globe, though for some, it will mean that, but it's a call to be missional in your movements and in your moments. Wherever you are going, as you go to work, as you go to school, as you go to the store, as you go to the gym; carry the Kingdom.

You don't need to wait for a "divine assignment" to appear in neon lights. If Christ is in you, then every space you enter becomes holy ground, not because of the environment, but because of the presence you carry.

The reason many believers feel stuck is because they're waiting for something spectacular, not realizing they've already been sent. The call to live on mission doesn't start with a passport or a platform, it starts with presence and obedience. Eyes open. Heart surrendered. Ears tuned in.

When you read the Gospels closely, you'll notice something profound: many of Jesus' most powerful Kingdom encounters didn't happen at the synagogue. They happened on the road, at the well, in someone's house, at a dinner table, or in the margins of everyday life. More happened on the way to the gathering or on the way home from it than inside the meeting itself.

Why? Because the Kingdom isn't a destination. It's a way of life.

This is what Jesus modeled: a life where every step, every conversation, every interruption was filled with eternal potential. And it's what He's calling us into.

Don't underestimate the power of presence.
Don't miss the holy hidden in the ordinary.
Don't wait to be used, walk as if you already are.

Because you are.
You've been sent and the Kingdom goes with you.

Living This Out

1. Wake with Purpose
→*Before you grab your phone or start your to-do list, take a moment each morning to surrender the day to Jesus.*
"Lord, as I go today, use me. Let me see people the way You see them."
Each day, no matter how mundane or busy, is sacred.

2. Walk Slowly Enough to Notice
→*Busyness blinds us to divine moments. Slow down. Pay attention.*
A smile, a question, or a simple act of kindness can open eternal doors.

3. Carry Christ into the Ordinary
→*Treat your everyday activities: Grocery lines, school pick-ups, and coffee*

runs as divine appointments waiting for a vessel.
Colossians 4:5 – "Make the most of every opportunity."

4. Listen for the Nudge
→*The Spirit doesn't always shout. Sometimes He whispers.*
Stay sensitive. The random thought, You should pray for them, might just
change a life.

5. Keep It Simple
→*You don't need to preach a sermon. Sometimes a listening ear, a shared*
story, or a word of encouragement is all it takes.
Jesus isn't saying, Go impress them. He said, "Go love them."

6. End Your Day With Reflection
→*Ask: Who did I love well today?*
Where did I sense God moving?
What might He be teaching me through today's moments?

Reflection Questions

1. Where has God already placed me "on mission" without needing to move an inch?

2. What would change if I truly believed I was sent?

3. How can I build rhythms of Kingdom purpose into my daily routines?

A Prayer for Living on Mission

Jesus,
You've sent me just as the Father sent You.
Help me see every moment as sacred, every place as a mission field.
I don't want to just go to church, I want to be the Church.

Give me eyes to see the need, ears to hear Your prompting, and a heart ready to love. Use my ordinary life for extraordinary Kingdom impact. Today, as I go, send me.

Amen.

If we're going to live on mission, we need more than passion.
We need perspective.
The clearest lens we've been given is Scripture itself,
But to see rightly, we must read rightly.
Let's rediscover how to read the Bible through the eyes of the King.

Chapter 7: Scripture Through the Lens of the Kingdom

"He explained... all the Scriptures concerning Himself." — *Luke 24:27, 45 (NIV)*

"You study the Scriptures diligently... yet you refuse to come to Me." — *John 5:39-40 (NIV)*

"He is the image of the invisible God... all things were created through Him and for Him." — *Colossians 1:15–20 (ESV)*

"In these final days, though, he spoke to us through a Son..." — *Hebrews 1:1–3 (CEB)*

"All Scripture is God-breathed and useful..." — *2 Timothy 3:16–17 (NIV)*

"The secrets of the kingdom of heaven have been given for you to know." — *Matthew 13:11*

The Lens That Changes Everything

Have you ever looked through a special lens that suddenly clarified what you were seeing? In a similar way, reading the Bible through the lens of the Kingdom brings the whole picture into focus. This "Kingdom lens" means viewing all Scripture as a unified story centered on Jesus Christ and His Kingdom. It's a perspective shift that changes everything. Instead of the Bible being a random collection of ancient texts or merely a manual of rules, it becomes alive. A window into God's grand narrative with Jesus as the King on every page.

On the road to Emmaus, two disciples experienced this firsthand. They knew the Scriptures, but they were confused and downcast until Jesus Himself joined them.

"And beginning with Moses and all the Prophets, He explained to them what was said in all the Scriptures concerning Himself" Luke 24:27 (NIV)

Suddenly, the seemingly disconnected stories and prophecies all pointed to one Person. Later, those disciples exclaimed how their hearts *"burned within"* them as Jesus opened the Scriptures to them (Luke 24:32).

When Jesus is the one interpreting, the Scriptures ignite our hearts.

This is the Kingdom lens at work, the realization that every chapter whispers His name, and every teaching unveils His character.

Without this lens, it's possible to read the Bible and completely miss the point. The religious scholars of Jesus' day knew the text by heart but failed to recognize the Author standing in front of them.

Jesus confronted them, saying, *"You study the Scriptures diligently because you think that in them you have eternal life. These are the very Scriptures that testify about Me, yet you refuse to come to Me to have life"* —John 5:39-40 (NIV).

In other words, they had the Scriptures but lacked the Kingdom perspective, the humble, open heart that seeks the King Himself.

All the Bible knowledge in the world is empty if it doesn't lead us to an encounter with Jesus.

Reading with a Kingdom perspective also means allowing the Holy Spirit to reveal the deeper meaning intended for Kingdom citizens. Jesus told His disciples, *"The knowledge of the secrets of the Kingdom has been given to you"* (Matthew 13:11). Others heard the same parables that Jesus taught, but didn't understand them, because they lacked the relationship and insight that Jesus gave His own.

Today, the Holy Spirit is our guide who opens our eyes (John 16:13–15). We begin to see how the *Old Testament* foreshadows Jesus and how the

New Testament reveals the fullness of His Kingdom. We start to connect the dots between prophecies, fulfillment, and our lives as believers in that Kingdom. The Bible turns from a puzzle into a picture of God's loving plan.

The Kingdom lens is not about finding new hidden codes or secret knowledge for a special few. It's about seeing the obvious reality that was there all along: Jesus is King, and *every* part of Scripture ultimately directs us to Him or flows from Him.

When this clicks, even familiar verses take on vibrant new color. The promises, the commands, the stories—all of them come alive because we see *who* they are pointing to and *what* they are drawing us into.

This lens changes not only how we read, but how we *live*. The Word of God ceases to be a distant text and becomes the voice of the King, inviting us into His life and mission.

Jesus Is the Centerpiece

In the Kingdom of God, Jesus is the centerpiece of everything, and Scripture is no exception. The entire Bible revolves around Him like planets around the sun. Paul writes that Jesus *"is the image of the invisible God"* and that *"all things were created through Him and for Him"* (Colossians 1:15–16).

He is the central figure holding all of creation and all of Scripture together. The writer of Hebrews echoes this by saying that while God spoke in many ways through the prophets in the past, *"in these last days He has spoken to us by His Son"* (Hebrews 1:1–2). Jesus is God's final and clearest message, the living Word to whom all the written words ultimately point.

It's possible, however, to treat the Bible like an end in itself and lose sight of Jesus. We shouldn't fall into the trap of pursuing Bible knowledge without pursuing Christ. We aren't just reading about Jesus, we are actively seeking and communing with Him in the Word.

In other words, every time we open the Bible, our goal is not to finish a chapter or check a study box, but to *meet the Lord*. To discover more of who Jesus is, what He cares about, and what He is saying to us today. This heart posture changes our Bible reading from a scholarly exercise into a relational adventure.

To be truly scriptural is to be Christological, because Jesus Christ is the subject of all Scripture. The Bible's true power lies in how it reveals Christ. Once we discover this truth, it changes our lives!

Think about that: Jesus is on every page in one way or another. He is the thread that ties every book of the Bible together in a beautiful tapestry. When we see Jesus as the centerpiece, the Bible's unity and purpose become clear. The stories of the Old Testament are not just history or morality tales; they set the stage for the coming King. The Gospels unveil Jesus in person, the Epistles explain life in His Kingdom, and Revelation shows Him as the triumphant King of Kings.

With Jesus at the center, even difficult or tedious passages find their meaning. The laws of Leviticus, for example, make sense when we see Jesus as our perfect high priest and sacrifice. The genealogy lists become thrilling when we trace the lineage of our Messiah. The prophecies sparkle when we realize they forecast the Messiah's mission. Every verse becomes a piece of a grand puzzle that, when assembled, reveals the face of our Savior. As we grasp this, reading Scripture transforms from duty to desire. We come not just to analyze a text but to encounter a Person and in meeting Him, we are changed.

Don't just read your Bible to find out what's wrong with you. Read it to see what's been made right through Him.

Kingdom Parallels Fulfilled in Christ

Throughout the Bible, we see a divine symmetry. Jesus fulfilling, reversing, and restoring what was broken in the Old Testament. These are more than coincidences; they are God's fingerprints in history, drawing all things into Christ.

Old Testament Event	Fulfillment in Christ
Adam fails in the garden	Jesus, the Second Adam, overcomes in Gethsemane (Rom 5:17–19)
Babel scatters the nations	Pentecost gathers the nations (Acts 2)
Sinai gives law on stone	Spirit writes law on hearts (2 Cor 3:3)
Temple houses God's presence	Believers become the temple (1 Cor 3:16)
Prophets speak in part	Christ is the full revelation (Heb 1:1–3)
Israel called God's son	Jesus, the true Son, fulfills their mission (Matt 2:15)
Sacrificial lambs cover sin	Jesus, the Lamb of God, removes sin (John 1:29)
Noah's ark saves a few	The Cross offers salvation for all (1 Pet 3:20–21)
Passover spares through blood	Jesus becomes our Passover Lamb (1 Cor 5:7)
Jonah in the fish three days	Christ rises on the third day (Matt 12:40)

And these are just a few of the many parallels we find. These divine patterns remind us that Christ is not a new addition. He is the long-awaited fulfillment.

The Bible is a unified story with Jesus at the center.

The Verse That Read Me

I used to approach my Bible reading the way I prepped for sermons — diligently, analytically, and, if I'm honest, sometimes with the goal of impressing others more than encountering God. I wanted to sound insightful, authoritative, polished. I prided myself on knowing chapters and verses, mastering timelines, and articulating doctrine with precision. Scripture became material for sermons, not a mirror for my soul. I was studying the Word to be heard, not necessarily to be changed.

But one day, a single verse flipped everything. It felt like the Bible started reading *me*.

The verse was John 5:39, where Jesus says, *"You study the Scriptures diligently because you think that in them you have eternal life. These are the Scriptures that testify about Me."* I had read that verse before, but this time, the next words stopped me cold: *"yet you refuse to come to Me to have life."*

In that moment, it was as if Jesus Himself was speaking straight to my heart. I saw myself in the religious leaders immersed in Scripture yet missing the One who it was all pointing to. Tears welled up. The Word I had handled for years was now handling me. My pursuit of knowledge had often eclipsed my pursuit of Him. I wasn't just studying anymore; I was being exposed. I closed my Bible and whispered a quiet, broken prayer: "Jesus, I don't want to preach about You without knowing You. I want to come to You."

That moment marked a turning point. I began to pray differently before opening the Bible: "Lord, show me You in Your Word. Let me see what You want me to see." Everything changed. The Scriptures stopped being a sermon source and started becoming a sanctuary. Passages that once felt dry or distant began to glow with meaning. I saw Jesus on the pages, His character, His love, His kingship in places I had skimmed right past before.

Reading the story of David and Goliath, I no longer saw just an underdog story; I saw Jesus the unlikely champion who defeated the giant of sin on our behalf. In the laws of the Old Testament, instead of mere rules, I began to see God's holiness and humanity's need for a Savior.

As I allowed the King and His Kingdom to become my lens, the Word of God read my life and transformed it. I remember coming across 2 Timothy 3:16–17 with fresh eyes: *"All Scripture is God-breathed and is useful for teaching... so that the servant of God may be thoroughly equipped for every good work."*

I realized then that God wasn't just filling my head with facts; He was equipping my heart and hands for Kingdom work. The Word was shaping me, not just informing me.

One morning, I was struggling to forgive someone who had deeply hurt me and probably contemplating ways I could deeply hurt them back. My natural instinct was to justify my anger. But that day, my reading plan led me to Matthew 18 and the parable of the unforgiving servant. As I read Jesus' words, I knew He was speaking directly to me. The story exposed my unwillingness to forgive. It felt like Jesus was sitting right beside me, gently saying, "This is about you. This is how My Kingdom works. Forgive, as you've been forgiven." With tears, I surrendered, and freedom flooded in. I was able to move forward with a debt-free heart!

Scripture, through the Kingdom lens, became more than a text. It became a personal conversation with God that read my heart and rewrote my responses.

I'm still on this journey, but one thing is clear: when we read the Bible with Jesus and His Kingdom in view, the Bible reads us, and we are never the same. The letter of the Word comes alive with the Spirit of the Word. It cuts and heals, corrects and encourages, calls out and calls forward. That one verse in John 5 was the wake-up call I didn't know I needed. It exposed my empty diligence and invited me into a living relationship.

Now, every time I open the Bible, I come as a disciple, not a preacher trying to impress, not a student trying to perform, but a son coming to hear from the Father. I don't ever want to go back to the old way. The

Kingdom lens has made all the difference. And the transformation it brings, is nothing short of life changing.

Kingdom Focus

All Scripture points to King Jesus
The Bible is not an end in itself; its purpose is to reveal Christ. From Genesis to Revelation, the central narrative is Jesus Christ: who He is, what He has done, and what He will do. When you know this, you begin to find Jesus in every story, prophecy, and poem of Scripture, either openly or in foreshadow. The whole counsel of God finds its center and unity in Jesus, so we read every part with an eye on the King and His Kingdom.

Relationship over religion
It's possible to be highly religious with Scripture and yet miss the relational heart of it. The Pharisees knew the text but refused the Person (John 5:39-40). The Kingdom lens keeps our relationship with Jesus front and center. We don't study the Bible to check a box or win an argument; we read it to know *Him*. This focus guards us from empty rituals. It turns study into intimacy, as the written Word always points us to the Living Word.

Revelation by the Holy Spirit
Understanding Scripture is not merely an intellectual exercise; it's a spiritual revelation. Jesus told His disciples that *"the knowledge of the secrets of the Kingdom"* was given to them (Matthew 13:11). In other words, God opens up truth to those who seek Him. The same Holy Spirit who inspired the Bible now illuminates it for us. Through prayer and intention, we invite the Spirit to "open our minds" (Luke 24:45) and shine light on the Word. With the Spirit's guidance, even familiar passages yield fresh Kingdom insights and previously hidden gems.

Scripture equips Kingdom living
When viewed through the Kingdom lens, even the challenging or obscure passages have *practical* purpose. Rather than reading for trivia or theory, we discover that Scripture is meant to shape our lives. *"All Scripture is*

God-breathed and useful," given to train and equip us for every good work (2 Timothy 3:16–17). That means each truth we learn is intended to be *lived out* in the love and power of God's Kingdom. We read, not to accumulate knowledge, but to be *transformed* into Kingdom people who carry out our King's mission.

The Kingdom Story – A Biblical Narrative

"Your Kingdom come, Your will be done on earth as it is in heaven." — Matthew 6:10

God's Master Plan to Reclaim the Earth

From the opening lines of Genesis to the final vision in Revelation, the Bible tells one unbroken story: the story of a King, His Kingdom, and His relentless mission to establish His reign on earth through a people who bear His image and carry His presence.

This isn't just a story of redemption; it's a story of reclamation. God's mission was never just to get people to heaven. It was always to bring heaven to earth.

Adam: The Kingdom Mandate Lost

In the Garden, God created humanity in His image (Genesis 1:26–28). Adam was not just the first man—he was the first representative of God's rule on earth. He was given dominion and responsibility. He was a royal steward of a physical realm meant to reflect a spiritual reality.

But Adam traded that Kingdom commission for self-rule. He chose autonomy over allegiance, and the result was exile. The Kingdom on earth was fractured—but not forgotten.

Noah: A Reset but Not Fulfillment

In a world overcome by corruption, God preserved a remnant through Noah (Genesis 6–9). The flood was a global reset a cleansing of creation. When Noah stepped out of the ark, God renewed the blessing: "Be fruitful and multiply and fill the earth" (Genesis 9:1).

But Noah, like Adam, would fall short. Though the earth was washed, the heart of man was still marred by sin. The Kingdom would have to come another way.

Abraham: A Family That Would Bless the Nations

God narrowed His plan to a single man, Abram, and through him, a nation (Genesis 12:1–3). The promise was Kingdom in scope: "I will make you a great nation... all peoples on earth will be blessed through you."

Abraham's descendants were to be a Kingdom of priests (Exodus 19:6), a holy people reflecting God's character and extending His rule. However, like Adam and Noah, faltered in their allegiance. The Law given through Moses exposed sin but could not restore hearts. The Kingdom had not yet come, but the King was on His way.

Jacob and the Twelve Tribes: A Nation Born, A Promise Continued

Through Jacob (Israel), God birthed the twelve tribes, the nation of Israel. They were chosen not for privilege but for purpose: to reveal what it looked like to live under God's rule. Through victories and exiles, prophets and kings, the message stayed the same: God wanted a people who would live under His reign and reflect His glory.

But even in the Promised Land, they chose kings like the nations around them and built altars to false gods. The Kingdom vision dimmed, but it never died.

Jesus: The King and the Kingdom Arrive

And then came Jesus. Not with a sword, but with a towel. Not with a throne, but with a cross.

Jesus is the second Adam (1 Corinthians 15:45), faithful where Adam failed. He resisted temptation in a garden (Luke 22:39–46), fulfilled the Law, and embodied the Kingdom.

His first words? *"Repent, for the Kingdom of heaven is at hand"* —Matthew 4:17 (ESV).

Jesus didn't come to announce religion. He came to inaugurate the Kingdom. Through His life, death, resurrection, and ascension, the King reclaimed the authority Adam lost and declared, *"All authority in heaven and on earth has been given to Me"* —Matthew 28:18 (ESV).

The Church: A People Who Carry the Kingdom

Jesus said, "I will build My Church (Ekklesia), and the gates of hell shall not prevail against it" (Matthew 16:18). That word—*ekklesia*—meant a governing assembly. Not a building or an institution. A called-out people living under the reign of the King and bringing His rule into every sphere of life.

Pentecost was never about an event alone; it was the reversal of everything broken. In Genesis 11 at Babel, human pride led to confusion of languages and the scattering of nations. Humanity's attempt to make a name apart from God ended in division. But in Acts 2, the Spirit came down and reversed the curse: every tribe and tongue heard the wonders of God in their own language. What was scattered in rebellion was gathered in redemption. What divided humanity was united in Christ. Pentecost is God reclaiming what Babel fractured; the birth of a Spirit-filled people who embody one Kingdom, under one King. The Church is now the beginning of that restored Kingdom; ambassadors of heaven walking on earth (2 Corinthians 5:20).

We are not just waiting for heaven. We are advancing the Kingdom.

The Consummation: The Kingdom Fully Come

The final vision in Scripture is not an escape from earth, but heaven descending down to earth (Revelation 21:1–4). The garden becomes a city. The dwelling of God is with His people. And the Lamb is the light.

Every tear is wiped away. Every enemy is crushed. Every tongue confesses: Jesus is Lord.

The Kingdom that was lost through Adam is fully restored through Christ.

Living This Out

Reading the Bible through the lens of the Kingdom is a practice we can cultivate daily. Here are some practical ways to live out this Kingdom-focused approach to Scripture:

1. **Begin with Prayer and Expectation**
   Don't rush into reading without God. *Pause and pray* before you open your Bible. Ask the Holy Spirit to reveal Jesus to you in the words you read and to give you a receptive heart. Approaching Scripture with an expectant, prayerful posture invites God to set the tone.
   Remember that you're not just reading a book; you're *meeting with the Author*.

2. **Focus on Jesus in Every Passage**
   As you read, intentionally look for Jesus and His Kingdom. In each story or teaching, ask yourself, where is Jesus in this? What does this show me about His character, His mission, or His Kingdom values?
   In the Old Testament, this might mean seeing how a character or event prefigures Christ (for instance, seeing sacrificial lambs as pointers to Jesus, the Lamb of God). In the Gospels, pay attention

to *how* Jesus speaks and acts as King, and what He says about the Kingdom.

In the Epistles, notice how every instruction ties back to the finished work of Christ or our life in Him. Keeping Jesus at the center of your reading guards you from getting lost in the weeds and keeps the main thing the main thing.

3. **Meditate and Let Scripture "Read You"**

   Kingdom reading is not a race; it's more like savoring a meal. After you read a passage, take time to reflect and listen. Meditation can be as simple as re-reading a verse slowly, emphasizing each word, or picturing the scene in your mind. Allow the Holy Spirit to highlight specific words or phrases. If something convicts you or shines a light on your life, pause and ponder it. You're not just studying; you're communing with Christ and being changed.

4. **Apply and Live the Word**

   After seeing Jesus in the Word and allowing that Word to examine you, respond with obedience. The Kingdom lens isn't fully in place until we *act* on what we see. You'll find your mindset and actions aligning more with the Kingdom of God – which is exactly what Scripture is meant to accomplish in us.

5. **Stay Consistent and Connected**

   Cultivating a Kingdom perspective is a journey. Over weeks and months, you'll notice your default way of reading has shifted to a more Christ-centered view. Share how God is revealing Himself in Scripture and listen to others' insights. Remember why you're reading: not to tick a box, but to know Jesus. Even on the days when inspiration seems lacking, your persistence is an act of love and faithfulness. Every moment in Scripture is an investment in your relationship with King Jesus.

By living out these practices, you'll find that reading the Bible becomes an adventure in partnership with God. Instead of a task, it feels more like walking and talking with Jesus on the road of life, just as those disciples did on the road to Emmaus. You bring your questions, He explains the way, and your heart burns within you with revelation and love.

This is the way of the Kingdom revealed in Scripture: a dynamic, life-giving encounter with the King through His living Word.

Reflection Questions

1. In my approach to Scripture, have I been more like a student collecting information or a disciple encountering Jesus?
   In what ways might I be "diligently studying" the Bible yet missing the Person it points to (John 5:39)?
   How can I shift my heart toward truly coming to Jesus through His Word?

2. Think of a Bible story or passage that has always puzzled you or seemed dry. How might viewing it through a Kingdom lens, looking for what it reveals about Jesus or His Kingdom change your understanding of it? What new insights about Jesus' character or work could be learned from that passage?

3. What is one practical step I will take this week to read the Word with fresh perspective?
   For example: Will I set aside a few extra minutes to pray before reading? Will I journal my reflections or discuss a scripture with a friend?
   Identify a step and commit to it, inviting the Holy Spirit to make the Word come alive as you follow through.

A Prayer to See the Word New and Fresh

Jesus,

Thank You for speaking to me through the Scriptures.

I confess that at times I've treated Your Word as common or approached it with a closed heart. Today I ask for fresh eyes. Let me look through the Kingdom lens that lets me see You on every page. Open my mind just as You opened the minds of the disciples, so that I can truly understand Your Word.

Jesus, I want to know You more intimately. As I read, let my heart burn within me with the fire of Your truth. Holy Spirit, be my teacher and guide. Reveal the secrets of the Kingdom to me as I seek You. Let Your word not just inform me but transform me. Make my life a living letter that reflects Your Word to the world. Lord, I treasure Your voice. Help me to come to the Scriptures with a childlike curiosity and a disciple's devotion. May Your Word always lead me to You, the King of kings.

Amen.

You've seen the seven priorities.
You've heard the call.
Now what?
The Kingdom life is something we step into.
Let's talk about where we go from here
and how to live this out with courage, clarity, and joy.

Chapter 8: The Kingdom Way Forward

"But seek first His Kingdom and His righteousness, and all these things will be given to you as well." — Matthew 6:33 (NIV)

"Seek first the Kingdom..." — *Matthew 6:33*
"Keeping our eyes on Jesus..." — *Hebrews 12:2*
"You are the light of the world..." — *Matthew 5:14*
"Our citizenship is in Heaven..." — *Philippians 3:20 (CEB)*
"Be transformed by the renewing of your mind..." — *Romans 12:2*
"Your Kingdom come, Your will be done..." — *Matthew 6:10*

Not Just a Teaching, A Way of Living

This book was never meant to be a theology textbook. It's not a manual for a better Christian life. It's a call to reorient everything around the reign of Jesus. I hope you will come back and revisit these priorities often. I encourage you to add your own thoughts and inspiration as you walk in the way of the kingdom.

The Kingdom isn't a side dish on the plate of our faith; it *is* the plate. It's the foundation, the framework, and the fuel. Now, it must become the way forward for your life.

You weren't just saved from something. You were saved *for* something.
You weren't just called to attend. You were called to advance.
You weren't just born again. You were born into a Kingdom.

Colossians 1:13 – *"He has rescued us from the dominion of darkness and brought us into the Kingdom of the Son He loves."*

What This Book Has Called You To

Let's not forget what we've walked through:

Christ-Centered Living – Jesus is not just Savior, He is King. Jesus is not just the starting point. He's the center, the substance, and the source. Everything flows from Him and points back to Him. (Colossians 1:18)

Kingdom Over Religion – We've traded performance for Presence. We reject man-made traditions and empty forms, not to become rebellious, but to reclaim the power and purity of the real Gospel. (Mark 7:13)

Discipleship Through Community – We grow best in authentic relationships. The Kingdom isn't lived out in isolation. We grow together, not through performance, but through shared life. (Acts 2:42–47)

Freedom from the World System – Our allegiance is to a better realm. We renounce the seductive pull of politics, consumerism, and cultural conformity in favor of eternal allegiance to our true King. (Romans 12:2)

Radical Grace and Repentance – Transformation flows from truth embraced. Grace isn't a license, it's a launchpad. True grace produces real change and invites us to turn from all that hinders love. (Titus 2:11–12)

Mission as a Lifestyle – Every moment is a holy opportunity. Kingdom people don't just support mission; they *are* the mission. Every table, workplace, and neighborhood becomes sacred ground. (2 Corinthians 5:20)

Scripture Through the Lens of the Kingdom – The Word is about a King, a Kingdom, and a called-out people. The Bible is not a rulebook or a weapon; it's a living invitation into the unfolding reign of Christ. (Luke 24:27)

These are not lessons to store away, they are realities to be lived out. Each of these priorities is a piece of a greater call: to live a life that looks like Jesus and reflects the rule of heaven on earth. The Kingdom way is not a program or a preference. It's a person. It's Jesus, lived out through His people, in every place, for all time.

Frank Viola once wrote: *"The Kingdom is not a place you visit, but a reality you embody."*

A Kingdom Way of Life

The call of Jesus isn't Come and learn. It's come and die. Then live again, new, free, sent.

A life lived under the rule of Christ is not perfect. It's not easy. But it is powerful. It's a life where love is stronger than fear, hope outlasts hardship, and joy doesn't depend on circumstances.

Romans 14:17 (CEB) – *"God's kingdom isn't about eating food and drinking but about righteousness, peace, and joy in the Holy Spirit."*

The Kingdom way forward looks like:

Choosing peace over panic (Philippians 4:6–7)
Choosing presence over performance (John 15:4–5)
Choosing obedience over comfort (Luke 9:23)
Choosing faithfulness over fame (Matthew 25:23)

> *Dan Mohler once said: "The Christian life isn't about surviving life, it's about manifesting Christ."*

A Kingdom People in a Compromised World

You are not called to blend in. You are called to break through.

The world doesn't need more sanitized, stage-ready Christians. It needs Kingdom people—fiery, faithful, filled with Jesus—living like He's alive and reigning.

Matthew 5:16 – *"Let your light shine before others, that they may see your good deeds and glorify your Father in heaven."*

You don't need a position to have impact.
You don't need a pulpit to preach.
You don't need applause to be effective.

You need conviction, you need clarity, and you need to remember who your King is.

1 Peter 2:9 (CEB) – *"But you are a chosen people, a royal priesthood, a holy nation, a people who are God's own possession..."*

The Mission Still Matters

Jesus has not changed His assignment:

"Make disciples of all nations..." — *Matthew 28:19*
"Go into all the world and preach the gospel..." — *Mark 16:15*
"Shine like stars in the sky..." — *Philippians 2:15*
"As the Father has sent Me, I am sending you." — *John 20:21*

This isn't a suggestion; it's a commission. The mission was never meant for a select few; but the everyday call for every Kingdom citizen. Wherever your feet take you, wherever your voice is heard, wherever your hands serve; *there* is your mission field.

The world doesn't need more polished events; it needs Spirit-empowered people. The office, the coffee shop, the gym, the dinner table, these are all platforms for Kingdom movement. You carry the Gospel not just in your words, but in your presence.

Christ in you is not just hope for you. It's hope for the world around you. The Kingdom is in you. Let it move through you.

A Vision for the Church Going Forward

So what does this mean for the Church?

What does it look like when God's people trade performance for presence, hierarchy for humility, and religion for reign?

The Church of the Kingdom is not measured by attendance, budgets, or branding. It's marked by presence, power, and participation.

It looks like this:

Every-member ministry (1 Corinthians 14:26): Everyone brings something. The pastor isn't the show, Jesus is. His Body is fully alive and fully engaged.

Christ as the actual Head (Ephesians 1:22–23): Decisions aren't made by preference or tradition but by discerning the will of the King.

Spirit-led gatherings: Order exists but not control. Plans are made, but space is left for the unexpected move of God.

Mission without walls: The Church doesn't gather to hide from the world; it gathers to be fueled for it. Monday matters just as much as Sunday.

Freedom from celebrity culture: The spotlight returns to Jesus. Leaders equip instead of dominate. The Body grows up into Him who is the Head.

This Church may not always look impressive from the outside. It may not trend or scale. But it will be fruitful. It will be faithful, and it will carry the fragrance of Christ wherever it goes.

Call to Courageous Allegiance

Living the Kingdom way will cost you.

Let's not pretend otherwise. You may lose friends. You may disappoint people who prefer religion over reality. You may be misunderstood or misrepresented. But you will gain something far greater: the King and His Kingdom.

Jesus was clear: the narrow road leads to life, but few find it (Matthew 7:14). He warned that following Him means dying to self, losing your life to find it (Luke 9:23–24). The call to follow the Lamb is not a casual invitation, it's a call to courageous allegiance.

"No one who puts his hand to the plow and looks back is fit for God's Kingdom." — Luke 9:62 (CEB)

Kingdom people are overcomers. Not perfect, not elite—just faithful. They keep showing up and they keep loving. They keep saying yes. Even when it's hard. Even when it costs them something.

"They were strangers and exiles on the earth... of whom the world was not worthy." — Hebrews 11:13, 38 (ESV)

You're not just called to believe in the Kingdom. You're called to live it, here and now, with courage and conviction.

The world may never understand it.
But heaven is watching.
And the King is returning.

Living This Out

1. **Crown Him Daily**
   Begin each day by surrendering your life to Jesus' reign.
   "King Jesus, rule my life today. I choose Your way."
   (Matthew 6:10)

2. **Anchor in Truth**
   Keep your heart tethered to Scripture. Let the Word train your
   thoughts and shape your vision.
   (Psalm 119:105)

3. **See with Kingdom Eyes**
   Look for divine opportunities in everyday places. Carry Christ
   into gas stations, boardrooms, living rooms, checkout lines.
   (Colossians 4:5)

4. **Don't Go Alone**
   Kingdom life isn't meant to be lived solo. Surround yourself with
   people who stir your fire and share your values.
   (Hebrews 10:24–25)

5. **Stay Sent**
   Wake up every day on mission. You've been sent. That doesn't
   change, so keep walking in it.
   (Isaiah 6:8)

Reflection Questions:

1. *What does seeking the Kingdom* first *look like in your daily
   life?*
   Are your priorities shaped by eternal truth or temporary convenience? Think about your time, your attention, your decisions. Is
   Jesus' rule evident in how you lead your home, manage your
   work, love your neighbors, and steward your influence?

2. *Where have you let comfort or fear steal your mission?*
   Are there places where the call of Christ has been replaced by the
   pull of safety? Have you delayed obedience because it felt

inconvenient, risky, or unpopular? What step of bold love or courageous truth-telling is He inviting you into now?

3. ***What would change if you lived like your life truly carried eternal weight?***
Imagine every word, every moment, every relationship charged with Kingdom significance. How would your conversations shift? Your prayers deepen? Your presence becomes more intentional? The light you carry is not small—it was made to shine.

A Final Prayer

Jesus,
You are the King. Let Your Kingdom come through my life.
Shape my thoughts, transform my habits, ignite my heart.
May I live with holy purpose, bold obedience, and unshakable joy.
Let me be a vessel of Your love. A citizen of Heaven.
A light in the dark. I don't want to just believe—I want to belong.
And I want to bring Your Kingdom wherever I go.

In Your name I pray,
Amen.

Appendix: Study Guide

Walking the Way Together

This study guide is designed to deepen understanding, spark honest conversation, and move the message of *The Way of the Kingdom* from pages into practice. Whether used alone, in small groups, or in a church setting, these questions aim to create space for reflection, alignment, and action.

Introduction for Group Leaders

This study guide is designed to help groups walk through *The Way of the Kingdom* together in a transformative and relational way. Each of the seven sessions corresponds to a chapter in the book and explores one of the seven priorities for Kingdom living. The structure includes Scripture, reflection, discussion, practical application, and prayer. Group leaders are encouraged to foster honest conversation, mutual encouragement, and space for the Holy Spirit to move.

Group Format Suggestions:

- Start with prayer and a brief time of connection

- Read the key Scripture aloud

- Share insights from the chapter

- Walk through the discussion questions

- Close with the "Practice This Week" and "Prayer Focus"

- Keep the tone grace-filled and Spirit-led

Session 1: Christ-Centered Living

Key Focus

Jesus is not just Savior—He is King.

Key Scriptures

- Luke 6:46
- Colossians 1:17–18

Summary

Kingdom life doesn't start with a church service, a moral checklist, or a better version of ourselves. It starts and ends with Jesus.

He's not just an idea we agree with; He's the One we revolve around. The gravity of His presence draws everything in our lives into alignment: identity, purpose, relationships, and even pain.

Living from the reality of Christ means we don't compartmentalize our faith. Jesus can't just be a part of your life. He *is* your life.

True surrender isn't found in striving, but in seeing. When we fix our eyes on Him, everything else finds its place.

Discussion Questions

1. What does it practically mean to have Christ at the center of your identity, decisions, and desires?
2. Where have you experienced "performance" over presence in your spiritual life?
3. Share a time when Jesus became more than an idea and became real to you.

4. What "good things" in life sometimes compete with Jesus for the center?

Practice This Week

Each morning, pause and pray: "Jesus, what would it look like to live today with You at the center?" Write the response and revisit it throughout the day.

Prayer Focus

Invite Jesus to take His rightful place at the center of your life. Surrender distractions and re-align your heart to His presence and leadership.

Session 2: Kingdom Over Religion

Key Focus

Allegiance to the Kingdom, not tradition.

Key Scriptures

- Matthew 15:8–9
- Colossians 1:13
- Matthew 23:13

Summary

Religion offers rules, but the Kingdom offers relationship. Jesus didn't come to start a new belief system—He came to inaugurate a Kingdom. Kingdom living means allegiance to Jesus, not to tradition, appearance, or performance.

Discussion Questions

1. How can we tell when our faith has drifted into religion instead of Kingdom reality?
2. Have you ever experienced "doing church" but missing the presence of Jesus?
3. What systems or habits have subtly shaped your faith more than Christ?
4. What does true allegiance to Jesus look like in your daily life?

Practice This Week

Identify one tradition or routine that may have become lifeless religion. Ask Jesus to breathe fresh Kingdom purpose into it—or stop it altogether.

Prayer Focus

Pray for a heart free from religious striving. Ask Jesus to expose any man-made filters in your faith and to renew your love for His Kingdom.

Session 3: Discipleship Through Community

Key Focus

Discipleship happens in shared life and experiences, not in structured programs.

Key Scriptures

- John 13:35
- Acts 2:42–47
- Hebrews 10:24–25

Summary

Discipleship was never meant to happen in isolation. It's forged in community—through relationships marked by love, accountability, and mutual transformation. Jesus didn't just teach disciples; He lived with them. The early Church didn't attend events, but they lived life together.

Discussion Questions

1. What has helped or hindered your experience of true community in the Church?
2. Why do you think discipleship thrives around tables more than stages?
3. What fears or excuses might be holding you back from deeper connection?
4. What could grow in your life if you were known and sharpened in community?

Practice This Week

Invite someone from your church or small group to share a meal or coffee. Ask them to share their story and listen without fixing, correcting, or teaching.

Prayer Focus

Ask God to lead you into deeper connection and to remove anything in your heart that resists vulnerability or mutual growth. Pray for courage to both receive and give love in community.

Session 4: Freedom from the World System

Key Focus

Live as citizens of heaven, not captives of culture.

Key Scriptures

- Romans 12:2
- John 18:36
- 1 John 2:15–17

Summary

The world system shapes how we think, what we value, and how we live—unless we choose the freedom of another Kingdom. Jesus didn't call us to blend in but to live set apart. Freedom comes not through effort, but by living under the rule of Christ and refusing the pressures of the world's system.

Discussion Questions

1. What does the "world system" look like in your everyday life?
2. In what ways have you been influenced by cultural values more than Kingdom ones?
3. What does it mean to live set apart—without becoming isolated or self-righteous?
4. Where do you feel most tempted to "fit in" rather than stand out for Jesus?

Practice This Week

Take a media fast (social, news, entertainment) for 24–48 hours. Use that time to listen to Scripture, journal, or sit quietly with Jesus. Notice how your perspective shifts.

Prayer Focus

Pray for discernment to see where the world's patterns have taken root in your mind or habits. Ask Jesus to rewire your desires and give you courage to live free and set apart.

Session 5: Radical Grace and Repentance

Key Focus

Grace empowers change; repentance is transformation.

Key Scriptures

- Romans 2:4
- Luke 15:17–24
- Titus 2:11–12

Summary

Grace isn't a pass to stay the same, but it's the power to live a new life. Repentance isn't just feeling sorry—it's a joyful turning toward Jesus. Together, grace and repentance create the atmosphere for transformation. When we say yes to His kindness, we step into resurrection life.

Discussion Questions

1. What's your current understanding of grace and how has it shifted over time?
2. How does the world's view of repentance differ from the Kingdom's view?
3. Why is repentance not just about behavior?
4. What does it look like to receive not just the forgiveness of Christ, but His life?

Practice This Week

Take 10–15 minutes each day to sit quietly and ask: "Jesus, is there any area where You are inviting me to turn toward You more fully?" Write down what He shows you and respond in faith.

Prayer Focus

Thank Jesus for His freely given and deeply transforming grace. Invite the Holy Spirit to lead you into joyful repentance wherever your heart needs alignment. Pray for eyes to see both the kindness of God and the power of His life in you.

Session 6: Mission as a Lifestyle

Key Focus

Mission is identity, not activity.

Key Scriptures

- Matthew 28:19–20
- John 20:21
- Colossians 3:17

Summary

Mission isn't a program or a trip—it's a lifestyle. When we understand who we are in Christ, we carry His presence and purpose into every space we occupy. Whether we're at work, home, or in the grocery store, we're on mission: loving people, sharing truth, and living the Kingdom visibly.

Discussion Questions

1. How has your understanding of "mission" evolved over time?
2. What might it look like to live as a missionary in your daily context?
3. In what areas of life do you find it most difficult to live missionally?
4. How does living on mission connect to your identity in Christ?

Practice This Week

Choose one space you inhabit regularly (workplace, school, neighborhood). Pray intentionally for the people there each day this week. Ask God for one opportunity to reflect Jesus through word or action.

Prayer Focus

Ask the Holy Spirit to awaken you to the people and needs around you. Pray for boldness, compassion, and clarity to live on mission wherever He sends you.

Session 7: Scripture Through the Lens of the Kingdom

Key Focus

Jesus is the key to understanding Scripture.

Key Scriptures

- Luke 24:27
- 2 Timothy 3:16–17
- Hebrews 4:12

Summary

To live the Kingdom life, we must see the Kingdom in Scripture. The Bible is not just a book of rules or stories—it's a revelation of the King and His reign. Reading through the Kingdom lens means we interpret everything through the finished work of Christ and the call to live as citizens of heaven.

Discussion Questions

1. How has your view of the Bible changed as you've grown in your faith?
2. What's the difference between reading for information versus transformation?
3. What does it mean to read Scripture with Jesus at the center?
4. Are there parts of the Bible you've struggled to understand or apply?
5. How can reading through the lens of the Kingdom bring clarity and joy?

Practice This Week

Choose one Gospel passage and read it three times this week, each time asking, "What does this reveal about the King, His Kingdom, and my response?"

Prayer Focus

Ask God to awaken fresh hunger for His Word. Pray for eyes to see Jesus, ears to hear His truth, and a heart to live what you read.

Leader's Wrap-Up: Finishing the Journey Together

As you complete these seven sessions, pause to reflect on what God has done in your group. Celebrate growth, transformation, and relationships that have deepened. Encourage each other to continue living these Kingdom priorities as a lifestyle.

Group Reflection Questions

1. Which session impacted you most deeply and why?
2. What area of your life has most shifted through this study?
3. How has your view of Jesus, the Kingdom, or the Church changed?
4. What spiritual practice or Kingdom value do you want to keep cultivating?
5. How can this group continue walking the Way together beyond these seven weeks?

Optional: Create a Kingdom Covenant

Invite each group member to write a short personal "Kingdom commitment"—a prayer, vision, or declaration that captures what God has stirred in their heart. Share them aloud or compile them into a document to celebrate your journey together.

Final Prayer Focus

Give thanks for all the Spirit has done. Pray for ongoing fruit. Ask God to seal what He started and lead each member into even deeper Kingdom living.

Commissioning Prayer:
King Jesus, we surrender again to Your rule. Shape our hearts to love what

You love, to go where You send, and to live as citizens of Your Kingdom. Let Your Kingdom come—through us, around us, and in us. Amen.

Bonus Resource: Weekly Journaling Page

You may wish to print or provide this simple page for each session:

Session Title: _____

One takeaway that stood out:

_____

One question I'm still thinking about:

_____

One thing I want to live this week:

_____

My prayer:

_____

_____

_____

Use this page during or after each session to track what God is doing in your heart.

Glossary

Abiding – Living in continual, conscious fellowship with Christ so that His life flows through the believer's words and actions (John 15:4-5).

Body of Christ – The spiritual family of all believers, each member uniquely gifted yet interdependent, with Jesus as the Head (1 Cor 12:12-27; Eph 4:15-16).

Citizenship (Heavenly) – The believer's primary identity and allegiance to God's Kingdom rather than earthly nations, systems, or cultures (Phil 3:20).

Community (Organic) – A Spirit-led, relational gathering of disciples where every member participates, versus a program-driven institution.

Covenant – A binding relational agreement initiated by God. In Christ believers enter the New Covenant of grace and indwelling life (Jer 31:31-34; Heb 8).

Disciple – One who intentionally follows Jesus, learns His teachings, imitates His life, and helps others do the same (Matt 28:19-20).

Ecclesia – Greek for "called-out ones"; the early-church word for a Kingdom assembly.

Freedom from the World System – Liberation from the values, powers, and loyalties that compete with God's reign (1 John 2:15-17).

Grace (Radical) – God's unearned favor and empowering presence that saves, transforms, and sustains the believer beyond self-effort (Eph 2:8-10).

Indwelling Christ – The reality that Jesus lives in and through His people by the Holy Spirit (Col 1:27; Gal 2:20).

Kingdom of God – God's active rule and realm, breaking into the present world through Jesus, ultimately consummated in the age to come.

Kingdom Lens (Scripture Through a) – Reading the Bible with the overarching theme of God's reign in view, rather than isolated doctrines or proof-texts.

Kingdom Reality – The authentic expression of the Kingdom's values—humility, service, love, power.

Lordship of Christ – Acknowledging and obeying Jesus as supreme ruler over every sphere of life, not merely accepting Him as Savior.

Mission as a Lifestyle – Viewing everyday environments—workplace, family, neighborhood—as the primary context for demonstrating and declaring the gospel.

Organic Leadership – Influence that arises from spiritual maturity and gifting rather than positional titles; leadership is shared and functional.

Repentance – A grace-enabled change of mind and direction—turning from self-rule to God's rule—that continues throughout the Christian journey.

Religious Drift – The subtle slide into routines, traditions, or mindsets that domesticate the gospel and substitute activity for intimacy with Christ.

Rest – Ceasing from self-effort to trust God's finished work, leading to inner peace and outward obedience (Heb 4:9-11).

Scripture Engagement – Immersing oneself in God's Word with the aim of transformation and obedience rather than mere information.

Shame Management – Attempting to appease guilt through works or image-maintenance rather than receiving God's grace and identity in Christ.

Spirit-Led – Directed and empowered by the Holy Spirit moment-by-moment instead of relying on formulas or fleshly initiative (Rom 8:14).

Transformation – The Spirit's ongoing process of conforming the believer to Christ's character and mission (2 Cor 3:18).

About the Author

Nathan Dennis is a follower of Jesus who has devoted his life to helping people discover what it truly means to live in the reality of God's Kingdom. He is passionate about guiding others into a deeper relationship with Christ and showing them that life with God is not about religious performance but about learning to live from His indwelling presence.

Nathan's heart beats for discipleship, authentic community, and spiritual renewal. Over the years, he has come to see that the Gospel is not simply a message we believe but a life we are invited to live, one in which heaven's reality begins shaping our everyday lives here and now. His desire is to help people not only know the truth but walk in it, moving beyond striving and into the freedom, identity, and purpose found in Christ alone.

Nathan and his wife, Sherry, share this journey together. They love creating spaces where people can encounter God's presence, build meaningful relationships, and discover who they were created to be. Family is deeply important to them, and they cherish time spent with their children while looking forward with joy and anticipation to the seasons still to come, including the hope of welcoming grandchildren someday.

They make their home in the mountains of East Tennessee, where they enjoy the beauty of God's creation, meaningful conversations with friends, and being part of what God is doing in their community. Above all, Nathan's hope is that through his writing and teaching, people will come to see that the Kingdom of God is not a distant concept but a present reality that transforms hearts, restores lives, and brings heaven's purposes to earth.

The Way of the Kingdom is the first in a series of books born from that calling. It is an invitation to live differently, to see differently, and to follow Jesus not only as Savior but as King.

Acknowledgments & Influences

First and foremost, I give thanks to the Lord Jesus Christ. Without His grace, guidance, and presence, my life would be meaningless. He is the Author of my story, the Light in my darkness, and the One who turns every page of my life toward His Kingdom.

To my family, Sherry, Chase, and Mackenzie; thank you for your unwavering love, patience, and encouragement. You have always been my motivation and my inspiration to keep moving forward. Your support has been the quiet foundation under every word written here.

To my mom and dad, words will never describe how grateful I am for everything you have done and been for me. I was a firsthand witness to you living out the priorities in this book every day. It has long been and remains my goal to make you proud.

While the words of this book are my own, the vision has been shaped through years of prayer, Scripture, and the influence of Kingdom-minded voices.

I am especially grateful for the teaching ministries of Dan Mohler and Frank Viola, whose lives and messages have helped me rediscover the simple, powerful way of Jesus and the call to live as Kingdom citizens today.

- **Dan Mohler** – Known for his Christ-centered teaching and emphasis on identity, righteousness, and practical transformation.
  Visit: www.fullyknownministries.com

- **Frank Viola** – A prolific writer and speaker focused on reclaiming the Gospel of the Kingdom and the organic expression of church.
  Visit: www.frankviola.org

Their teachings have inspired not only my personal walk, but many of the truths explored throughout these pages.

www.ingramcontent.com/pod-product-compliance
Lightning Source LLC
Chambersburg PA
CBHW032228080426
42735CB00008B/767